# AMOS ALONZO
# STAGG

# AMOS ALONZO STAGG

COLLEGE FOOTBALL'S MAN IN MOTION

JENNIFER TAYLOR HALL

*Foreword by Jerry Markbreit*

THE
History
PRESS

Published by The History Press
Charleston, SC
www.historypress.com

First published 2019

Manufactured in the United States

ISBN 9781467145220

Library of Congress Control Number: 2019947298

*For Uncle George*
*Thank you for every story.*

*Leave me no compromise on things half done, keep me with a stern and stubborn pride, and when at last the fight is won, God keep me still unsatisfied.*[1]

—*Amos Alonzo Stagg*

# CONTENTS

# Contents

# FOREWORD

I met the Grand Old Man of Football in 1956. Shortly after my graduation from the University of Illinois, I was invited to attend a clinic for prospective football officials at the University of Chicago. The guest speaker at this wonderful gathering of prospects was the legendary football coach who had led the University of Chicago's football team for over forty years. Every man in the audience sat with rapt attention as the ninety-two-year-old spoke of his love for the great game. Following his presentation, I couldn't believe my good fortune at being able to meet him and tell him of my aspirations.

Alonzo Stagg was the most important man in developing our wonderful game of football as it is today. I say this with some authority by virtue of my close association with football over the past sixty-one years. My first introduction to Mr. Stagg came in 1955 during my junior year at the University of Illinois in the School of Physical Education. Amos Alonzo Stagg's name appeared numerous times throughout the curriculum. I became interested in what he had accomplished, but at the time, he was only a name. My short-lived attempt at playing Big Ten football led me to begin officiating intermural football. I loved the game and loved the challenge. After my graduation, I joined an officiating group to learn as much as I could. As I sit here, reflecting on my long career on the field, I credit the life and outstanding accomplishments of Alonzo Stagg and especially, the personal encounter we had in 1956.

Alonzo Stagg was a great athlete as a young man who fell in love with the game of football. One result of his contributions is that many football events today bear his name, including the Division III Championship Game—the Stagg Bowl—and the Big Ten Conference Football Championship game, which awards its winner the Stagg Trophy. His impact on college football is unequalled.

I was fortunate to have felt his impact personally. His strong influence on me made my officiating life more successful than I could have ever imagined. After ten years of high school and small college football officiating, I joined the Big Ten Conference, where I worked for eleven years. Then I moved on to the National Football League for twenty-three years. I served as head referee of the NFL for twenty-two of my twenty-three years, and I was honored to officiate four Super Bowls.

Thank you, Mr. Stagg, for allowing me to work for so many years in the game that I love because of your great love and contributions to the best sport in the world.

—Jerry Markbreit

# PREFACE

**C**oach Amos Alonzo Stagg's accomplishments on the gridiron and his service to the institution of college football define his life and legacy. But his enduring influence on the men who played for him is the heart of his story.

I have been asked many times why I decided to write a book about a football coach of a bygone era. The answer, in part, is the story of my love for the game and its heroes, and it begins in Starkville, Mississippi. This is where I spent every Christmas of my childhood. In my family, it was an accepted truth that the only place to be on Christmas morning was at Aunt Martha and Uncle George's house. Santa expected you to be there, and that's where he was delivering your gifts. That's where we celebrated faith and family. And we filled up on food and football.

Watching football with Uncle George, a former NCAA and NFL running back, was a trip to Disney World with Mickey Mouse as my guide. He knew—or was somehow connected to—at least one man in every game we watched, it seemed.

And he always had a story. Many were set at Ole Miss or Delta State, where he played college football, and some in Miami, where he spent three seasons as a Dolphin; but regardless of the setting, I hung on every word. He brought football to life, filling in the broadcasters' sketches with bold strokes of vibrant color.

He helped me understand and appreciate the game—that what great players made to look easy was far from it. Most of his stories left me roaring with laughter, and a few opened my eyes to the unwholesome side of the game, but they all left me wanting to know more. More about the game's history and how it became a thread in the fabric of our society. More about the players and coaches who bring its history to life.

My quest for more led me to Amos Alonzo Stagg. His remarkable life and enduring legacy are the story I have the privilege to tell.

# ACKNOWLEDGEMENTS

**T**elling the story of Mr. Stagg's life and legacy became a reality with the help of many people.

Mr. and Mrs. Stagg catalogued their life in articles, photographs, personal and professional correspondence and a variety of memorabilia. And Stella Stagg saved *everything*. For that, I am enormously grateful. With the help of the accommodating staff at the University of Chicago Special Collections Center, I was allowed to see her handiwork, all archived as the Amos Alonzo Stagg Papers.

I use the term *their* deliberately, because coaching was not his dominion alone. As every man who played for Mr. Stagg at the University of Chicago, the College of the Pacific and Susquehanna University would attest, Stella Stagg earned the title "Greatest Assistant Coach." Her painstakingly detailed play charts, her thorough pre-game scouting, her exhaustive play-by-play notes and her concise post-game analysis were second to none.

Another smaller collection of Stagg artifacts is located at Susquehanna University in Selinsgrove, Pennsylvania. During my visit there, Chris Markle, the university's senior development officer, provided VIP access to me and to my traveling companions: Coach Wayne Hardin, Dr. Joe Morelli of Temple University and Ms. Joan Haefle. Joan was the ringleader of our visit to her beautiful alma mater, and she is a woman whose ability to bring people together and make things happen rivals that of a head of state. Thank you, Chris, for planning and conducting a wonderful tour—Susquehanna couldn't find a better ambassador! Thank you also to Dr. Pam Samuelson,

Susquehanna's former athletic director; Katie Meier, the director of athletic communications; and Mary Sanders, the university's archivist, for your support of this book.

Amos Alonzo Stagg High School in Palos Hills, Illinois, also houses a small collection of Stagg memorabilia. Jennifer Baniewicz, the collection's curator, aided my research by unearthing videos and photographs and sharing them with me. Thank you, Jenny, for going beyond what your job requires to help me. The Archives and Special Collections of Springfield College in Springfield, Massachusetts (formerly the International YMCA Training School), contains rare Stagg photographs and writings. Thank you to Jeffrey Monseau, the college archivist, for providing me access to these valuable pieces of memorabilia and for your words of encouragement.

Thank you to the late Wayne Hardin, who welcomed me into his Pennsylvania home and shared his memories of the Staggs and their role in shaping his success as a player, a coach and a man. We developed an easy rapport and sealed our new friendship with a pan of homemade cornbread—proof that you can take the boy out of Arkansas, but you can't take Arkansas out of the boy.

Thank you to the late Kristie Crisler, who shared memories and cherished family photos of her grandfather Fritz Crisler, the University of Michigan coaching legend who credited his success to the influence of Mr. Stagg. Kristie served as my research assistant at the Bentley Historical Library at the University of Michigan and enthusiastically cheered me on in this endeavor.

I owe my deepest gratitude to the Stagg family. Barbara Stagg Eccker opened her Michigan home to me and gave me full access to all of her family's cherished photographs and papers. She, her husband, Jack, and her cousin Paul "Skip" Stagg Jr. all shared stories and personal reflections of their grandparents Stella and Alonzo Stagg.

To all of you who are intimately connected to the people whose stories fill the pages of this book, thank you for sharing your loved ones with me. My great hope is that I have honored them by telling their stories well.

I am thankful to God for giving me the opportunity to write this book. My prayer is that people who are not familiar with the contributions of Mr. Stagg—particularly those of my generation—will come to know him for what he accomplished on the gridiron, for his service to college football and for his effect on the men who played for him.

Thank you to my editor, Bill Ecenbarger, for sharing a veteran's wisdom with a rookie author. You taught me that if outlining is easy, I'm not doing it right. You also parceled out the perfect amount of encouragement to keep me in the ring.

Thank you to Ben Gibson and The History Press for seeing the merits of Mr. Stagg's story and taking the plunge with me to tell it.

To my mother: Thank you for teaching me at a young age that a good book is a great companion. To my father: Thank you for being my biggest cheerleader and for taking to the open road with me on my interview journey. And to both of you: Thank you for filling your girl's childhood with opportunities to enjoy the great game. To Mike: Thank you for tolerating the constant presence of my laptop. To Fletcher, Thomas and Everett: Thank you for cheering me on and putting up with all that was required of our family to make this book a reality. Your curiosity and encouraging words provided the spark I needed at just the right time. To my girls: Thank you for never letting me forget I could do this. And to my Aunt Martha: I'm so glad you said "Yes" to Big George. I hope I have made you all proud.

# AUTHOR'S NOTE

Since I began working on this book four years ago, my goal has been to tell the story of Mr. Stagg through the prism of the world he changed—capturing the spirit of the man, describing the effect of his innovations on the game of football and making him known through individuals changed by his formative influence. His legacy lives in the game he devoted his life to and through people whose lives he touched.

In the course of my research, I was fortunate to meet and interview people who knew Stella and Alonzo Stagg. I leaned heavily on them to verify specific accounts from newspaper articles, books and other source material.

In the absence of a direct quote or firsthand recollection, I have retold events based on a compilation of sources. In some instances, I have taken creative liberties to craft dialogue, but the retelling remains faithful to the spirit of the individuals and the setting of the events.

# INTRODUCTION

On August 16, 1862, President Abraham Lincoln was preparing to issue the Emancipation Proclamation, the transcontinental telegraph had just begun carrying messages from the Atlantic coast to the Pacific, and in West Orange, New Jersey, Eunice Pierson Stagg gave birth to her fifth child, Amos Alonzo.

Amos Lindsley Stagg worked as a shoemaker, providing for his wife and children using the craft he learned as a seven-year-old apprenticed to a cobbler after his mother's death. Demand for shoes was often inadequate to sustain the large family, so the Stagg patriarch found work in all manner of physical labor. Young Amos Alonzo ("Lonnie," as his parents affectionately called him) helped the family by cutting heavy, wet hay in the Newark salt meadows and threshing grain with hand tools. Lonnie relished the physical labor, which produced a chiseled physique. That same work instilled in him a reverence for self-discipline and self-reliance—qualities that would form the pillars of his character. It also honed the coordination that combined with his strength and agility to enable his success as an athlete.[2]

From a young age, Lonnie Stagg gravitated to the game of baseball. The gridiron grass on which he would establish his legacy was just beginning to take root on college campuses and had not found a home in American preparatory schools. The Staggs' home of West Orange had no high school, but neighboring Orange allowed non-resident enrollment at its high school by charging tuition. Lonnie's Sunday school teacher encouraged him to enroll, so the industrious teen took on additional work beating carpets, cleaning stoves and mowing lawns to pay the tuition. He performed well in the classroom and even better on the baseball diamond, where he established a reputation as an ace pitcher. As Lonnie prepared to graduate, Orange High's assistant principal, Alton Sherman, persuaded him to enroll at Yale to further his education.[3] To any other student, Sherman's encouragement would have seemed quixotic, as less than 2 percent of the population attended college at the time.[4]

Stagg sat for Yale's entrance exam but was unable to pass, so he enrolled in preparatory school at Phillips Exeter Academy in New Hampshire. With only twenty-two dollars in his pocket, he rented an unheated garret room—his home for the duration of his stay at Exeter. Stagg became a standout on the school's baseball team, establishing a reputation "that put the recruiting agencies to work," as his son, Alonzo Jr., would describe it decades later.[5]

The seeds of his faith, which were nurtured at the First Presbyterian Church of Orange, compelled Stagg to embrace the virtues of a strong mind, body and spirit as he prepared for the next chapter in his life. But the financial struggles of his family were never far from his thoughts.[6]

Stagg enrolled at Yale University as a divinity student in the fall of 1884, and with no athletic scholarship and little financial help from his family to cover expenses, he worked as a campus custodian and waiter to pay his $1.00-per-week rent, $0.20-per-day meals and $29.80-per-semester tuition.[7]

Stagg's pitching skills secured him a starting position on the varsity baseball team his freshman year. During that first season, he led the Elis to a 2–1 victory in an exhibition game with the Boston Braves.[8] Stagg's reliability on the mound kept him in the role throughout his career at Yale, and during his tenure, the team earned five consecutive championships behind his 34-8-1 record. With no limits on eligibility,[9] Stagg played each of his years as a Yale undergraduate and graduate student.

On May 26, 1888, the first lady of the United States stood witness as Stagg imprinted his indelible mark on college baseball by striking out twenty Princeton batters while allowing only two hits.[10] Asked later about his epic performance, Stagg replied, "Mrs. Cleveland entered the grandstand wearing the orange and black of Princeton. As the wife of the President of the United States, it seemed to me that she should have been neutral, and I pitched my arm off in resentment."[11]

Four weeks later, on June 23, Yale faced Harvard for a share of the league championship. Stagg took his position on the mound, and Yale won, 8–0. The two teams met for a deciding game three days later. With his arm too numb to pitch using his typical wind-up, Stagg opted for an underhanded delivery.

He induced seventeen fly outs and led the Yalies to a 5–3 championship win over the Crimson.[12] During Stagg's five years on the mound, Yale went 15-4 versus Harvard and 14-3 versus Princeton.[13]

Stagg first played football during his third year at Yale and then sparingly, as the baseball captains feared he would injure his pitching arm.[14] Notwithstanding his limited role, Stagg established himself as a leader on the gridiron team. In 1888, a college rule change lowered the tackling line from the waist to the knees, and Yale players struggled to adjust. Stagg responded to the problem by rolling up a mattress and hanging it from the roof of the gym. He then laid additional mattresses underneath as cushions and ran his teammates through long tackling drills. Stagg's tackling dummy emerged as the first of many innovations he contributed to the game of football.[15]

After two years of occasional service at end and guard, Stagg began to play regularly as a graduate divinity student. In 1889, he, Pudge Heffelfinger and Charles O. Gill led the Elis to a 15-1 record, and the three were named to the first All-America team by Caspar Whitney and Walter Camp.

As Stagg continued his graduate studies in religion, he began to doubt his ability to influence others for Christ as a preacher. Despite all of his success in athletic pursuits, he lacked confidence in public speaking. In 1890, Alonzo Stagg left Yale and his pursuit of the ministry. Realizing he could best serve the Lord influencing men on the gridiron and other fields of competition, he enrolled at the newly opened International YMCA Training School in Springfield, Massachusetts. There he began his coaching career. And there, Alonzo Stagg apprenticed for his life's calling as an architect of football and a builder of men.

## Chapter 1

# ECKIE

**W**alter Eckersall lay motionless beneath the crisp white sheet. Not asleep, but not fully awake. Morning rounds were underway, and the muffled sounds of a conversation in the adjacent room could be overheard through the thin walls.

"The incision is healing properly. Ambulation should begin today."

"Continue phenacetin."

"Three hundred milligrams, four times per day?"

"Yes. Resume normal diet in the absence of dyspepsia."

As the voices faded to silence, Eckersall rolled onto his back, expecting the medical entourage to greet him next. The door to his room opened on its creaky hinges, and Eckersall's eyelids slowly separated to reveal two small, dark circles set in a hazy yellow matching the hue of his skin.

In the glow of the hallway's light stood the figure of a man at least four inches shy of six feet but with broad shoulders and thick hands that hinted at the honed physique beneath his twill suit.

"Mr. Stagg?" Eckersall eased himself up in the bed. "I thought you were the doctor."

"Hello, Eckie. Not a doctor," the Old Man quietly laughed. "May I come in?"

"Yes, sir. Of course," said Eckersall as he tried to remember the last time he had seen his former coach.

He couldn't recall the date but guessed it was during a game he had officiated the previous fall. The former Maroon star regularly worked as a football official in addition to his job as a sportswriter for the *Chicago Tribune*.

The enterprising Eckersall also worked occasionally as a paid game publicist for Knute Rockne. The Notre Dame coach frequently provided Eckersall with game tickets in addition to his compensation, which the shrewd Eckersall would sell for a tidy profit, providing him the opportunity to quadruple dip on a single game.[16]

Alonzo Stagg stood at the foot of Eckersall's bed. "Son, you know I had to come and see you."

"Mr. Stagg, I'm sorry I haven't paid you back the twenty dollars you loaned me so long ago." The ailing man's jaundiced cheeks flushed with shame. "I haven't forgotten how you helped me out of a jam, and I intend to repay my debt to you."

"Eckie, I'm not here to collect debts," Stagg responded. "But regarding that jam you got yourself into…"

"Yes, sir," the player interrupted. "I'm sorry about that too."

Stagg did not know any details of the incident under discussion other than that one of his boys had violated two of his cardinal rules. One of those sins—profiting off the amateur game—was reprehensible to the man who revered the sport as a molder of men. Eckersall's second violation of Stagg's credo threatened not only the men's relationship but also Eckersall's life.

"You are going to turn over a new leaf now, aren't you?"

"Yes, sir. I am," Eckersall replied. "My doctor says if I don't, it'll kill me."

Stagg looked at the man who, just over a decade earlier, was widely regarded as the greatest football player of his era. Behind his elusive speed and keen instincts, Chicago lost only two games during Eckersall's three years as the Maroons' starting quarterback.[17] Now the all-time All-America's body wore the scars of hard-lived years following his departure from the Midway campus.

Eckersall's carousing had become a thing of legend in the Chicago sports community, and years earlier, Stagg had counseled his beloved former pupil to change his ways. Despite Eckersall's embarrassment at his coach's reproach, however, the young man continued on his errant path. Eckersall went so far as to join a tobacco company's national advertising campaign, an egregious violation of Stagg's rules against smoking and exploiting athletics for personal financial gain. Eckersall added these violations of the Stagg code to his excessive drinking and achieved the trifecta of transgressions.

Stagg ardently believed that the damage wrought by alcohol and cigarettes far outweighed any momentary pleasure they offered—a tenet of his orthodoxy that emerged from his father's decision to remain temperate.

Public drunkenness was prevalent in the Staggs' rough West Orange neighborhood, even among the parents of his friends. The marked contrast of Amos Lindsley Stagg's example was not lost on his young son, who as a famous football coach years later would describe his father as "superbly honest and just."[18]

Alonzo Stagg also considered the practice of trading on one's name "odious."[19] He was approached on countless occasions with offers to be paid as an athlete or as a product pitchman, and he refused each time.

"You kept me on the straight and narrow path, Mr. Stagg. But I've strayed far from it," Eckersall confessed as he hung his head. "You kept us all on the right way."

"You're right that I taught you better," agreed Stagg. "But when you were at Chicago, what did I say to you boys about successful plays?"

"Repeat them," Eckersall replied.

"Eckie, you have a second chance here. You know the play. Now you repeat it."

The door opened again. "Mr. Eckersall, my name is Dr. Kutzler. I…," he stopped as he looked up from the chart to see the patient and his visitor.

"Oh, hello, Coach Stagg." Kutzler immediately recognized the famous coach and extended his hand to greet him.

"A pleasure to meet you, sir. I know you're taking good care of our boy here."

Stagg walked to the door and looked back at the Maroon star. "Behave yourself, Eckie."

*Chapter 2*

# TRIBUTE

**F**rom the window of his Cobb Hall office, William Raney Harper stared at the muddy field where Chicago's Maroons had humiliated the University of Texas, 68–0, two weeks earlier. As snowflakes fell on the gridiron, Harper recalled his hope that the victory would invigorate his ailing friend. But in November 1904, the forty-two-year-old Alonzo Stagg struggled to rebound from the pneumonia and rheumatism that had plagued him throughout the fall. As the football season drew to an end and the coach's illness lingered, a growing concern surrounded the normally ebullient Stagg.

Harper returned to his roll-top desk and picked up his pen.

> *He came; he was given every opportunity he desired, and as a result, it is not too much to say that western athletics have been altogether transformed....*[20]
>
> *Knowing, as I do, that athletic sport is one of the most important agencies in contributing to the ethical uplifting of young men in college, and realizing, as I do, the splendid work in this direction which Mr. Stagg has accomplished, I rejoice (1) that he has lived, (2) that being such a man, he has given his life to college athletics, and (3) that the field of his work has been Chicago and the University of Chicago.*[21]

Fourteen years earlier, with the promise of a "palace car and a vacation," Dr. Harper had courted Alonzo Stagg to join him as the first athletic director and head football coach at the University of Chicago.[22]

Harper, previously a Yale Divinity School professor, was tapped in 1890 to lead the midwestern university founded by John D. Rockefeller. The philanthropic industrialist and the school's first president envisioned a liberal arts institution offering numerous fields of study to a wide array of students—a profound contrast to the schools of theology that dominated the academic landscape in late nineteenth-century America.

Harper believed physical education and athletics were integral to a well-rounded education, and he persuaded the university's regents to support the appointment of an athletics director with faculty standing. In the fall of 1890, he contacted Stagg, his former student, and invited him to a meeting in New York.[23]

"I want you to join me in Chicago, Alonzo." Dr. Harper wasted no time in making his pitch. As the two men met over breakfast at the Murray Hill Hotel, the conversation remained largely one-sided.

"This is your opportunity to build a program. You will be in charge of the athletic department and the football team. All of it will be yours to develop." Eager to persuade his former student to move to Chicago, Harper launched into a salary negotiation. "The university will pay you $1,500 a year."

The twenty-eight-year-old Stagg thoughtfully considered the proposal. Harper waited impatiently for a response, increasing the offer as the silence lingered.

"Two thousand dollars a year. And an assistant professorship."

As Stagg sat silently, Harper made his final offer to close the deal. "The university will give you an annual salary of $2,500 and an associate professorship. That's an appointment for life, Lon."[24]

Harper was not the first prospective employer to encounter gridlock in negotiating with Stagg. In 1888, six National League baseball teams fought for Stagg's services. The Boston Braves offered Stagg, still a poor Yale University student, $3,000 a year to leave college and play professional baseball. Stagg declined, and Boston raised the offer to $5,000 a year. The New York Nationals asked him to play a three-month season for $4,200.[25] At the time, Stagg was living on $1.50 per week and rationing food when he ran out of money. Stagg refused the ballclubs' offers, declaring that his conscience would not allow him to sell his services and abandon his alma mater.[26] Years later, he reflected on the life-changing decision: "I never did a wiser thing than refusing the $4,200 a season offered me by the New York Nationals in the '80's, when that sum just about represented the national wealth to me. If it is money the college man wants, he ought to be able to make more on a real job than by peddling a physical skill."[27]

Stagg's conscience proved to be the harbinger of his destiny.

Not long after he declined the professional teams' advances, Stagg entered Yale Divinity School to prepare for a career in the ministry.[28] It was there that he enrolled in a Hebrew class taught by Dr. William Rainey Harper.

Stagg left an indelible impression on Harper with his performance in class, on the baseball diamond and on the football field. So, when the newly minted university president went in search of someone to head the University of Chicago's athletic department, Stagg was his first choice.

"Two thousand, five hundred dollars a year. Faculty standing with a lifetime appointment. The entire athletic department—not just football—under your purview."

Harper waited for Stagg's answer. "What do you say, Lon?"

Neither the salary nor the promised fringe benefits, however, persuaded Stagg to leave the YMCA Training School (now Springfield College) to move to the Midwest and serve as Chicago's athletics director.

Stagg at last responded to Harper's proposal: "I'll come if you let me combine athletics and physical education in one department."

A few days following their meeting, Alonzo Stagg confirmed his acceptance in a letter to Dr. Harper, declaring, "After much thought and prayer, I feel decided that my life can be best used for my Master's service in the position which you have offered."[29]

"I kept thinking it over. I suppose Dr. Harper thought it was money. It wasn't at all," Stagg recalled years later. "While Dr. Harper was talking during that breakfast, I was wondering if Chicago would be a better 'field to till' than the East."[30]

In the months prior to his meeting with Harper, Stagg had made the life-changing decision to end his pursuit of the ministry to study physical education. After repeated unsuccessful attempts at delivering sermons while at Yale, Stagg realized he was unfit to preach from the pulpit. The man who had devoted years to studying and preparing for the ministry was paralyzed with anxiety when he stood to speak formally before a large audience.

"How can I spread the Word of God if I cannot speak?" Stagg agonized.

In time, he came to realize that he did not need a pulpit to preach his message. Stagg reasoned, "Every man can, and should, do what he is best qualified to do, but in such a way that his principles shine for all to see. Ministers are ambassadors for Christ; so can all men in all professions be." For Alonzo Stagg, that profession was athletics. If he could influence athletes doing what he had hoped to do as a minister, would he not be reaching the same goal?[31]

In 1890, Stagg embarked on a new journey: studying physical education at the International YMCA Training School. When he accepted Dr. Harper's offer to join the University of Chicago faculty, Alonzo Stagg took the next step of his odyssey—one that would begin in the fall of 1892 and lead him to an unparalleled career coaching young men on the gridiron of the Midway.

Stagg's appointment at Chicago set a precedent in the selection of athletic directors in American universities, not simply for the salary and tenure that accompanied it. Harper and Stagg developed an intimate, lifelong friendship whose impact transformed athletics at the University of Chicago and brought about a sea change in intercollegiate athletics throughout the United States. "It was evident that Stagg had certain ideals about athletic work and of athletic policy, and he made it clear that his coming to Chicago was dependent wholly upon his having every opportunity to work out those ideals."[32]

Harper continued his obituary for Stagg:

> *I do not mean to say there would have been no change in these twelve or fifteen years in western college athletics if Mr. Stagg had not come to Chicago. This, of course, would be absurd. But I do mean to say Mr. Stagg has contributed to this transformation more than all other agencies combined. His intense love for pure sport, his incorruptible spirit, his indefatigable effort, his broad minded zeal and his absolute fairness of mind and honesty of heart have exerted an influence upon western university and college athletics that has been felt far and wide and produced results of which we may all reasonably be proud. I am myself of the opinion that great progress has been made in these dozen years; and if this is true, no one will fail to ascribe at least a large portion of credit for this to Mr. Stagg.*[33]

The *Chicago Daily Tribune* published Dr. Harper's tribute on November 20, 1904, alongside an editorial listing Stagg's numerous accomplishments. The *Tribune* also noted the many expressions of sympathy Stagg received from all over the country.

The Grand Old Man's obituary, as it turned out, was published prematurely. Coach Amos Alonzo Stagg died on March 17, 1965, in Stockton, California. He was 102.[34]

Chapter 3

# YMCA

**T**wo years prior to his move to Chicago, Alonzo Stagg entered the International YMCA Training School to prepare for a career in coaching and physical education.[35] There he coached and played on the football team—unofficially dubbed "Stagg's Stubby Christians"—who took on anyone willing to schedule them. The squad finished Stagg's first year with a 5-3 record, including a narrow loss to East powerhouse Yale— quite a feat for a school with forty-two students.[36] The December 12, 1890 contest between Stagg's squad and his alma mater was notable for its venue as much as for its outcome: Madison Square Garden hosted the two teams in football's first indoor game.[37]

While at the YMCA, Stagg brought innovative thinking to the game as he considered new formations to counter the size and skill deficits of his players. In 1890, he developed the ends-back formation, pulling his ends back from the line, using them like backs to carry the ball around the opposite ends and drive into the line ahead of the ball carrier.

"At Yale, I had perceived that I could do more effective work as interference for the runner by lining up slightly behind the line of scrimmage as an end. So at Springfield I pulled my ends back from the line and used them as running and blocking backs," Stagg recalled. From the ends-back formation, Stagg derived ten crisscross plays—now collectively known as the reverse.[38]

Soon after arriving in Springfield, Stagg met a McGill University graduate named James Naismith. Stagg recruited the 154-pound Naismith to play center on the football team, despite the availability of a 195-pound teammate—a choice that when Naismith himself questioned, Stagg explained simply, "Jim, you seem to do the most diabolical things in the most gentlemanly manner."[39]

Like Stagg, Naismith had planned to become a minister. His love of athletics, however, diverted his path to the YMCA college, where he sought to make physical training his life's work.

In the fall term of 1891, YMCA superintendent Dr. Luther Gulick assigned Naismith a project whose result would write its creator into the history books. Dr. Gulick summoned the young instructor to his office on an early December morning to discuss a new pursuit for their charges.

"I have a job for you, Jim. No one seems to know what to do with these boys once the mercury falls." The head of the school looked at the young coach. "And we need to keep them fit through the winter. I want you to take that class and see what you can do with it. You've got two weeks to come up with a new game to keep those boys busy."

Naismith took his marching orders and retreated to his small office above the gymnasium's locker room. There, bent over his desk, he deconstructed the elements of familiar sports and children's games. As Dr. Gulick's deadline loomed, Naismith wracked his brain for the elusive answer.

Fourteen days later, he stood at the door, staring at the gymnasium floor below. Naismith grabbed a soccer ball and ran down the stairs.

"Mr. Stebbins!" he called across the gym, his words echoing off the wood floors. The custodian of the school's buildings looked up from his hammer and nails as the young coach ran toward him. "Mr. Stebbins, do you have two square boxes, about eighteen inches on each side?"

"No boxes," replied the older man. "But I'll tell you what I do have. Two old peach baskets down in the storeroom, if they'll do you any good." Naismith followed Stebbins to the storeroom and grabbed the baskets. "Come with me. And bring that ladder," Naismith nodded toward the corner of the room.

At each end of the gym, on the lower rail of the balcony ten feet above the floor, Naismith nailed a peach basket. On the bulletin board, he posted a list of rules. Borrowing from lacrosse, rugby and "duck-on-the-rock" (a boyhood game of his Canadian hometown), the young player-coach created the new game just under Dr. Gulick's deadline.

The following day, Naismith gathered his players to unveil his invention. As his charges filed into the gym, Naismith held up the ball and succinctly explained the object of the game.[40]

"The idea is to throw the ball into the opposing team's basket," Naismith said as he pointed to each end of the gymnasium. He divided them into two teams of nine men, tossed the ball into the assembled group and blew the whistle.[41]

What transpired was decidedly more rugby than modern-day basketball. The list of injuries included multiple black eyes and a separated shoulder. When Naismith blew his whistle to end the contest, one player lay unconscious on the gym floor. The young coach returned to the drawing board to modify the rules, hoping to eliminate the brawling.

"After the free-for-all we had yesterday, I changed the rules a bit," said Naismith as he scanned the bruised and bandaged group the next morning. "No more running with the ball. And no striking it with the fist, or holding, tripping, pushing or shouldering an opponent."[42]

After several days of experimenting, the coach and players discussed additional adjustments to the game, including cutting out the bottom of each peach basket—this at the request of the man assigned to remove the ball after each successful shot.[43]

Naismith also felt compelled to reconsider his original name for the new sport; he had intended to call his invention "box ball," but the shape of Mr. Stebbins's donations to the effort rendered that imprecise. He eschewed calls to name the game for himself—"A name like 'Naismith Ball' would kill any game," he famously protested—instead agreeing with those who suggested "Basket Ball."[44]

In his role as a player-coach at the YMCA, Alonzo Stagg participated in the early basketball games with his colleague Naismith. History shows the game's inventor played in only two games—one a 1–5 loss with Stagg responsible for the team's lone score. In the effort, Stagg also fouled every player on the opposing side.[45]

In the days that followed the inaugural games, laughter and shouting from inside the YMCA's gymnasium piqued the interest of passersby, and the young men soon found themselves playing their contests before crowds of spectators. Many were teachers from a nearby public school, who, after witnessing the new sport, wanted to organize their own teams.

"Consequently," basketball's inventor recalled years later, "women were playing the game within a month after our first efforts."[46]

The sport that effortlessly crossed gender lines soon migrated west with Naismith's friend and colleague Stagg. "We'll see what Dr. Harper has to say about making basketball players of our football boys," said Stagg, as he thought of keeping his prospective athletes physically fit through winter in the Midwest. "Can you teach them to score more and foul less than you?" Naismith chided his friend.

When Stagg left Springfield for Chicago in 1892, he took Naismith's game with him, establishing a Maroon basketball team that he coached along with football, baseball and track. During basketball's early years, Stagg suggested reducing each side from nine players to five, and on January 18, 1896, he coached the first intercollegiate basketball game featuring teams of five.[47] His Maroons defeated the University of Iowa, 15–12.[48] Stagg's efforts in the Midwest and Naismith's work in the East grew basketball's popularity, and within a few years, intercollegiate competition existed throughout the country.[49]

When asked years later about his father's involvement with the new game, Alonzo Stagg Jr. stated, "The YMCA often sent boys away for publicity, and my father was away during the first official basketball game. My father and Dr. Naismith were very good friends, and my father contributed to development of the game but was reticent to take credit for anything he didn't originate."[50]

As a member of the YMCA student-faculty, Alonzo Stagg served as an ambassador for the school with civic and religious groups. He was not entirely comfortable in the role of public speaker but consented to perform the task when called on by the school's administration. On one occasion, Stagg and Dr. Gulick traveled to a convention at Williams Bay near Lake Geneva. After Stagg delivered a speech to the assembled crowd, he overheard Dr. Gulick remark to a colleague, "Isn't it too bad Staggie can't speak?"[51] Following his return to the Springfield campus soon after the trip, Stagg attended a church service in which a fellow classmate delivered a particularly inspiring sermon. The events reinforced for Stagg that he was not suited for the ministry, and he determined instead that he could influence men for God from the sidelines rather than the pulpit.

James Naismith continued his work in Springfield until 1895, when he and his wife, Maude, moved to Denver. He enrolled in medical school and taught at the local YMCA college. In 1898, they moved to Lawrence, Kansas, and he began teaching physical education, coaching basketball and serving as chaplain for the University of Kansas. Naismith would go on to serve as the university's physician and athletic director.

By Naismith's sixth season on the Kansas hardwood, his teams had finished above .500 only one year. As the game's inventor famously told his protégé, Phog Allen, "You can't coach basketball. You just play it."

Perhaps Naismith knew of what he spoke: the game's inventor holds the ignominious distinction as the Jayhawks' only coach with a losing record, carrying a mark of 55-60 during his nine seasons leading men on the Kansas hardcourt.[52]

Allen dismissed Naismith's pronouncement, and in 1907, the future Hall of Famer accepted Kansas's offer to be its head basketball coach. In contrast to his mentor, Allen succeeded in spectacular fashion, amassing a school-record 590 wins over thirty-nine seasons in Lawrence.

Their coaching records notwithstanding, basketball's inventor and one of its legendary coaches remain forever linked in the annals of the game and at the home of Jayhawk basketball: Naismith Court inside Allen Fieldhouse.

In his later years, Naismith recalled the highlight of his life as his attendance at the 1936 Olympics in Berlin, where basketball was played as an Olympic sport for the first time. To honor the game's founder and his approaching retirement, the National Association of Basketball Coaches had conducted a nationwide fundraiser to finance Naismith's trip to Germany.[53]

During the second week of February 1936, every American high school, college and university was asked to designate one game as the "Naismith Game." Participating schools donated one cent from each admission, and the organizers used the collection to fund the trip. The generosity of basketball fans from coast to coast provided Naismith $4,700 to witness the historic ten-game international competition.[54]

Before the tournament games began, players from the competing nations honored the game's inventor at the Berlin stadium.

"When I walked out on a Springfield, Massachusetts playground with a ball in my hand and the game in my head, I never thought I'd live to see the day when it would be played in the Olympics," Naismith responded to the crowd in his characteristically humble manner.[55]

In the final game, the United States defeated Canada, 19–8, on an outdoor dirt court.[56] Rain fell throughout the contest, transforming the playing surface to mud and slowing the game from a sprint to a slog, prompting one observer to comment that "the game might have been better if it had been played under water polo rules."[57]

But there, in the shadow of war and alongside the iconic American track stars led by Jesse Owens, basketball found an international following, as its inventor looked on with delight.

Stagg home, West Orange, New Jersey. Birthplace of Amos Alonzo Stagg, August 16, 1862. *Courtesy of the Stagg family collection.*

Amos Alonzo Stagg, age ten, with older brother George Randolph Stagg, age twenty-two. *Courtesy of the Stagg family collection.*

*Above*: A young Stella Robertson, undated.
*Courtesy of the Stagg family collection.*

*Right*: Stella Robertson, 1891. *Courtesy of
the Stagg family collection.*

*Above*: Phillips Exeter Academy
baseball team (1883–84).
*Third row, standing, left to right*:
Williams (catcher, third base),
Stagg (pitcher, third base),
Jennison (catcher, pitcher).
*Second row*: Honoré (right field),
Durant (center field), Cook
(substitute), Foss (first base).
*First row*: Moulton (left field),
Gill (second base), Wurtenburg
(shortstop). *University of Chicago
Photographic Archive, apf1-07861,
Special Collections Research Center,
University of Chicago Library.*

*Right*: Alonzo Stagg class
picture at Yale, 1888. *Courtesy
of the Stagg family collection.*

Members of the 1888 Yale University baseball team, Amos Alonzo Stagg (*right*), pitcher, and Jesse Chase Dann (*left*), catcher. *University of Chicago Photographic Archive, apf1-07791, Special Collections Research Center, University of Chicago Library.*

*Left*: Amos Alonzo Stagg playing baseball at Yale, undated. *Courtesy of the Stagg family collection.*

*Below*: Yale University championship football team of 1888. *Third row, from left*: Billy Rhodes (right tackle), George Woodruff (right guard), William "Pudge" Heffelfinger (left guard), Charlie Gill (left tackle), Fred "Kid" Wallace (left end), Billy Bull (fullback). *Second row*: Amos Alonzo Stagg (right end), Lee "Bum" McClung (right half), William "Pa" Corbin (captain, center). *First row*: William Wurtenburg (quarterback), Billy Graves (left halfback). *University of Chicago Photographic Archive, apf1-07804, Special Collections Research Center, University of Chicago Library.*

YMCA baseball team, 1890. *Front row, left to right*: J.M. Dick, W.D. Barry, G.H. Finch. *Middle row*: W.J. Keller, W.H. Ball Jr., A.A. Stagg (captain), Thomas Scotton, A.E. Garland. *Back row*: A.P. Stockwell, James Naismith (manager), B. Van Leuvan, W.O. Black. *Courtesy of Springfield College, Babson Library, Archives and Special Collections.*

YMCA's 1890 football team (known as "Stagg's Eleven"). *Top row, left to right*: W.J. Kellar, James A. Naismith (inventor of basketball), J.P. Smith, D.W. Corbett, W.O. Black, W.H. Barton. *Bottom row*: W.C. McKee, F.N. Seerley, Amos Alonzo Stagg (captain), A.E. Garland, W.H. Ball. *Courtesy of Springfield College, Babson Library, Archives and Special Collections.*

## Chapter 4

# THE UNIVERSITY OF CHICAGO ERA BEGINS

**W**hen William Rainey Harper hired Alonzo Stagg as athletic director and head football coach at the University of Chicago, academic standing for coaches was unheard of, and the entire academic world viewed the appointment with some skepticism.[58]

Alonzo Stagg arrived at his post on the Midway with his workplace still under construction. He recalled, "When I reported for duty in September 1892, no building had been completed and the carpenters were still at work on Cobb Hall, the one structure nearing completion."[59] To say the coaching genius who became the "Grand Old Man of Football" started from scratch is an understatement the length of a few football fields.

On October 1, Stagg issued his first call for football players. Thirteen showed up and were so underwhelming that the thirty-year-old coach had to leave the sidelines and join them on the field. But with the game still in its infancy, the notion of a player-coach was not viewed as particularly unusual.[60] The rookie squad won its opening game a week later, 14–0, versus Hyde Park High School. Chicago's first match-up with a collegiate opponent came against Northwestern on October 22. The schools battled to a scoreless tie, but in the process, Chicago collected its first football revenues—$22.65 as its share of the gate receipts.[61]

Professor Stagg stressed his commitment to the amateur code in collegiate athletics in a speech on campus later that month. He promised, "We will not hire men to come to the university because they are athletes nor will we pay their expenses there because they are athletes," a practice he contended eastern schools had engaged in for years.[62] With equal passion, the head coach rallied Chicago students to cheer on their football team. Many of the university's students did not understand the game, as it was not played in their hometowns, so Stagg's rallies were often educational in nature.

At a campus Halloween party that fall, he offered a football primer to the assembled revelers. One of the co-eds in attendance was a freshman from Albion, New York, named Stella Robertson. The seventeen-year-old member of the women's basketball team was a quick study of the gridiron game, and she impressed the young coach with her curiosity and insight. The two began to spend time together as a shared love of athletics grew into a courtship. After watching the Lady Maroons on the court later that year, the smitten Stagg described Stella as "a scrappy girl who could play basketball under men's rules"[63]—high praise from one of the game's pioneers.

On the gridiron, Stagg established himself early on as a champion of fair play and an honest broker of the game. When an injury in practice prevented the young coach from participating in Chicago's November 24 contest with Illinois, Stagg was asked by Illini officials to referee the game.[64] He did. No complaints were heard from the crowd gathered in Champaign for the Thanksgiving Day match-up—other than the cries of disappointment from the Chicago faithful whose Maroons' 12–28 loss brought a disappointing end to the season.[65]

Chicago's 10–4 defeat of Illinois on November 11 represented its only victory against a major opponent in its opening season. The Maroons won 7 contests against non-major (high school and YMCA) teams and finished their first gridiron campaign with a record of 8-4-1.[66]

Harper and Stagg were eager to build on growing interest in the game, recognizing the benefits that would accrue both to the football team and to other less marketable campus sports. With that in mind, Harper solicited a gift of land near the Chicago campus to be used for home football games.[67] The wealthy Chicago merchant Marshall Field agreed, and he leased land to the university that became the football field bearing his name.

In Chicago's second season, Stagg only scheduled games against other colleges and universities. Chicago opened the 1893 campaign with contests against nearby Lake Forest College and Northwestern University, then hosted the University of Michigan on October 21. Following their 10–6 victory over the Wolverines, the Maroons traveled to Lafayette, Indiana, for a date with Purdue on October 25. Stagg's only quarterback was sidelined by injury, forcing the coach to suit up and play behind center. In what was described as a "battle royal from the start" that required the home team "to strain every muscle," the Purdue eleven defeated the Maroons, 20–10.[68] The game was so hotly contested that before it ended, the Tippecanoe County district attorney marched onto the field and threatened to issue indictments for assault and battery.[69]

Chicago finished its second year with a 6-4-2 record and boasted wins over Cincinnati, Michigan, Northwestern and Notre Dame.[70]

That same year, Stagg and Minnesota head coach Henry Williams (a Yale teammate) published *A Scientific and Practical Treatise on American Football for Schools and Colleges*—the first book on football to include diagrams of plays.[71] This encyclopedic text offered the unschooled fan—a vast majority of the game's spectators at the time—a thorough explanation of football's ways and means.

Stagg continued to reshape the game with the innovative alignments and plays he devised in his football laboratory on the Midway. In 1894, he began placing the quarterback to receive the ball from center in a standing position as in modern T-formation.[72] According to Stagg, "It not only saved the moment lost in rising from a stoop but it minimized fumbles by permitting the quarterback to use his body as well as his hands in taking the ball from center."[73]

In Chicago's November 29 game against Michigan, Stagg unveiled his tackles back formation. With the ball just beyond midfield, the Chicago offense lined up with tackles George Knapp and Charles Roby pulled back behind the line. As Andrew Wyant snapped the ball to Frank Hering, the tackles swept left and met the Michigan right tackle. Hering tossed the ball to right halfback Frederick Nichols, who followed his blockers around the Wolverine right end for a quick ten-yard gain. Maroon left halfback Harry Coy and left end Henry Gale followed with a series of short gains up the middle. Then, with the ball inside the Michigan one-yard line, Gale took the handoff from Hering and plunged through the Michigan defense for the game's first score. On Chicago's next possession, Nichols followed his tackles around Michigan's right end for a thirty-yard gain. Stagg called his name again, and Nichols delivered an end run of twenty yards, but the normally sure-handed halfback fumbled the ball at the Michigan five-yard line just as the Maroons appeared poised to score. Late in the second half, Michigan then ran its version of the end-around with left halfback Gustave Ferbert scampering around the Chicago line for a seven-yard score. The late touchdown and successful 2-point kick sealed a 6–4 victory for the Wolverines.[74]

Chicago's third year of football also marked the genesis of the passing game. After observing his quarterback Frank Hering throw the football with a baseball pitcher's motion, Stagg conceived plays in which Hering made a long *lateral* pass to an end when receiving the opposing team's kicks.[75]

"Hering could throw a tight spiral. Other boys curled the ball against the forearm and threw it out with a sidearm pass. But Frank's instincts told him the ball would travel further and more accurately if he threw it with an overhand motion,"[76] Stagg said in praise of his quarterback years later. Hering's lateral passes figured prominently in Stagg's playbook, but the coach's use of the forward pass remained confined to the practice field for more than a decade, until the play was legalized by the Football Rules Committee.

## Chapter 5

# THE HONEYMOON

William Rainey Harper envisioned athletics as "a vital part of the student life…a real and essential part of college education,"[77] when he hired Alonzo Stagg as the University of Chicago's first athletic director and football coach. At Chicago, under the direction of Professor Stagg, every student participated in compulsory physical education coursework. But in Dr. Harper's view, football was the first among equals. In addition to its curricular benefits, football served the unique function of promoting the university beyond the confines of the Midwest. For the nascent university, such an advancement tool was invaluable. So Harper implored his football coach to "develop teams which we can send around the country and knock out all the colleges."[78] Stagg shared Harper's belief in intercollegiate athletics—particularly football—as a unique publicity tool and was eager to expand the university's reach with it.

Motivated by the challenge of the university president, Stagg readied his men with contests against regional foes such as Michigan and Northwestern, and at the first opportunity, he put his men to the test on a national stage.

Throughout the first three weeks of December 1894, Stagg negotiated terms of a post-season contest between the Maroons and the Cardinal[79] with H.S. Hicks of Leland Stanford Junior University (now Stanford University). After exchanging dozens of telegrams, the men settled on dates and revenues for each school. In the end, Chicago agreed to play two games against Stanford and one game against the Reliance Athletic Club of Los Angeles.[80] To help offset travel expenses, Stagg scheduled a fourth game: on their return home, the Maroons would stop in Salt Lake City for a match-up with the city's YMCA football squad.[81]

Stagg described the trip as a "transcontinental football pilgrimage." Without question, it heralded a new era in the evolution of college football.[82]

At the same time Stagg accepted Harper's charge to the football program, Chicago's coach also took him up on the promised "palace car and a vacation." The end of the Maroons' regular season freed Stagg and his new bride to leave Chicago and enjoy a delayed honeymoon during the school's Christmas break. Aboard the railcar *Georgia*, Stella Robertson and Amos Alonzo Stagg embarked on a cross-country trip three months after their September 10 wedding.

The newlyweds arrived in San Francisco on December 23 with seventeen football players in tow.[83]

In a pre-game interview with the *San Francisco Call* newspaper, Alonzo Stagg embraced the historical significance of his team's excursion as he divulged the unpremeditated nature of its origins. "This is the first extended tour of any football team, but I think it will be the setting of a fashion that will be widespread. I told the boys as a joke that if they beat Michigan, I would take them to the coast. Michigan won against us in the last few minutes of a game that had been ours from the start. The men did so well, and my suggestion had so taken hold of them that I telegraphed Stanford's director of physical education, whom I knew personally, asking him if a game could not be arranged, and the thing was done."[84]

The games with Stanford represented college football's first post-season, neutral-site play—contests that would usher in the era of bowl games. For her part, Stella Stagg was not about to miss football history in the making. She would have ridden cross-country in a horse-drawn wagon to share the experience with her new husband and the men of Chicago.

Unfortunately, the *Georgia* was not a vast improvement over an Old West Conestoga. On the second night of their journey, Alonzo Stagg awoke with a cough. Gray smoke filled the cabin, burning his throat and filling his nostrils. "Stella, get up. The train is on fire." Stagg's characteristically calm voice delivered the urgent message.

The train's upper berths had collapsed before the travelers reached the Iowa state line the previous night. Then, as they continued their journey through the Rockies, the Chicagoans awoke to discover the car on fire.

Stagg met two of his defensive linemen in the passage. "Get to the dining car and fetch some water. We need to douse this fire." The train toiled on, upward through the mountains, as the engineer, the brakeman, the fireman, the cook, two newlywed passengers and their seventeen charges battled the blaze from an overheated coal stove that ignited the surrounding woodwork.

In Sacramento the following day, the erstwhile firefighters transferred to a regular Pullman car that provided safe passage for the final leg of their journey to San Francisco.

Rather than broadcast their travails to a Bay-area newspaperman, the Maroons' captain, Charles W. Allen, instead described the journey as "a picnic."[85] He went on to explain the manner in which he and his teammates maintained their enthusiasm on the cross-country journey. "We have played football in about six states since last Wednesday, and the team was never in better form. At every station where the train took any kind of a breathing spell, we piled out and had a run, and if the stay was long enough, we took the ball and went through a bit of signal practice. It was quite entertaining for the rest of the passengers, I've no doubt. In the evenings when it was too dark to practice, we would entertain everyone with college songs and a yell or two."[86]

Having safely arrived at their destination, the Maroons continued preparations for their December 25 date with Stanford at Haight Street Grounds, site of the first "Big Game"[87] between Stanford and the University of California two years earlier. Haight Street provided a venue for the Chicago versus Stanford football contest—as well as the first four meetings between Stanford and Cal—but its origins were in baseball. The historic San Francisco park was built in 1887 for the California League and served as its home until the league disbanded in 1893.[88] Tragically, the great earthquake of 1906 destroyed the landmark located on the east side of Golden Gate Park.

From the opening kickoff of the Christmas Day contest, the men of the Midway battled a strong foe in the Walter Camp–coached Stanford team. Camp, already a football giant, began his second stint as the Cardinal head man in the fall of 1894. A decade prior, the legendary Camp had coached Stagg at Yale, and much of the pre-game publicity focused on the match-up between the two Elis.[89]

The clock wound down on the first half, and the battle of attrition prepared to yield the game's first score. As the players emerged from a goal line pile, referee Will Pringle (head coach of the Reliance Athletic Club) judged the Maroons to be short of the end zone in their fourth down attempt. The teams ran off the field, and Chicago quarterback Frank Hering approached umpire Warren Olney Jr. to protest his colleague's call.

"You all are favoring Stanford. Don't rob us!" Hering implored.[90] Olney answered the claim of bias with a fist to Hering's jaw. Chicago's quarterback then delivered a response to Olney's nose, ushering a tidal wave of Chicago and Stanford players into the mix. Several police officers quickly broke up the brawl and dispatched the teams to their locker rooms, preventing additional carnage.

A local newspaperman described the teams' first-half play as "a model exhibition of excellent football tactics."[91] Stagg, however, did not share the media's favorable assessment of his team's opening performance and delivered a thorough dressing-down of his men at intermission. "Boys, you look like you're asleep out there. I expect you to snap out of your trance and play like this means something to you,"[92] declared the frustrated head coach.

As the second half got underway and the Northern California temperatures began to drop, the Chicagoans hit their stride. The Maroons took the opening kickoff and marched down the field with ease. A sideline observer noted that on the first series, "Gale [Chicago's left end, Henry Gale] was pushed through the center as if the Stanford men were made of putty."[93] Moments later, Chicago's Clarence Herschberger stole around the end for a touchdown. Addison Ewing quickly followed with another touchdown, and the Maroons led, 12–0. On two successive plays, Stanford blocked Herschberger kicks, but during the second attempt, Maroon right halfback Frederick Nichols scooped up the fumbled ball and ran seventy yards for a touchdown.

The Maroons' second-half play revealed a marked difference in the two teams' level of preparation. A well-conditioned Chicago squad dominated the line and exploited the fatigue of Stanford's eleven. When the final whistle signaled the end of play, a euphoric Maroon team celebrated its 24–4 Christmas Day victory before the crowd of four thousand spectators. Stella Stagg kept account of every play for Chicago and its opponent, a practice she repeated in the three games that followed and that she continued throughout her husband's career.[94]

The teams met for a second game in Los Angeles, where Stagg and Hicks hoped the Southern California venue would attract additional spectators— and the accompanying gate receipts. The Los Angeles Amateur Athletic Club hosted the rematch on a rainy and humid December 29.

Walter Camp's men rebounded from their earlier drubbing by the Maroons and gave the nearly 4,500 Cardinal faithful plenty to cheer.

From the opening play, the Maroons struggled to gain their footing. "They look like they're pulling anvils out there!" Stagg exclaimed as his backs were bogged down in the muddy trenches. "Did the Stanford boys plow the field to plant their crops?"[95] Stanford's defense kept Chicago from reaching the goal line, while its offense managed to score two touchdowns before time expired.

A Chicago sweep of Stanford was not to be. The muddied and spent Maroon squad fell, 12–0, as Stanford exacted revenge for the 20-point beating the team had suffered four days earlier.[96]

Stagg's Maroons boarded a San Francisco–bound train and returned to Haight Street Grounds on January 1 for a meeting with the Reliance Athletic Club of Oakland.[97] No written accounts indicate whether Stagg discussed the earlier difference of opinion between his quarterback and Reliance's head coach (referee Will Pringle) as the team prepared to face its New Year's Day opponent.

Reliance boasted two key advantages over Chicago: size and experience. The Pacific Coast champion squad was composed of former college players who outweighed their Windy City counterparts by an average of twenty pounds per man.

A crowd of five thousand welcomed the new year while gathering to witness the emerging sport that had found its way west.[98] Eight years later, the first bowl game—the Tournament of Roses East–West football game— would be played in Pasadena, instituting a New Year's Day tradition that continues to this day.

Clear skies and mild temperatures provided an ideal backdrop for the afternoon contest. Chicago received the opening kickoff and gradually worked its way to midfield before surrendering a turnover and forty yards to Reliance. The men of Oakland scored quickly, a mere ten minutes into the first half. For the remainder of the afternoon, the two teams battled in the trenches and traded punts. Their solid tackling notwithstanding, the Reliance men skirted the bounds of sportsmanship, sidelining both Andy Wyant and Emery Yundt of Chicago with late hits to the head. Stagg's men likewise sent two opposing players to the ground with injuries in a contest that resembled a bitter conference rivalry rather than a first meeting of intersectional opponents.

Despite Chicago's improved play in the second half, Reliance's physical dominance and skill proved insurmountable in the mud-soaked trenches of the San Francisco field. With a 6–0 loss, the Maroons completed the California series and readied themselves for their final game and the journey home.

On January 4 at 2:30 p.m., Stagg and his boys arrived at the Salt Lake Exposition Grounds for a date with the city's YMCA team. The Maroons exposed the home team's inexperience in a contest played in snow, slush and freezing temperatures. Salt Lake had no answer for the brilliant play of Chicago's Nichols and Allen, who led their team to an 18–0 halftime score. The visitors went on to score at five-minute intervals throughout the second half, on their way to a 52–0 pounding of Salt Lake. By five o'clock, the Staggmen had finished their business on the gridiron and were aboard the eastbound train home.

Back on the *Georgia*, the misfortunes that had plagued the westward trek continued on the return to Chicago as repairs to a flattened wheel stalled the train in Laramie, Wyoming. While they waited, several players went hunting and supplied the chef with fresh jackrabbit for their dinner's main course. Coach and Mrs. Stagg opted for steaks, but as an homage to victorious hunters—and perhaps in honor of the historic journey— Mrs. Stagg carefully preserved the tablecloth stained with the spoils of the hunt.[99]

When they arrived home safely after two weeks of travel, the Staggs learned that their purportedly luxurious private railcar had been used by traveling minstrel shows in its previous life, prompting Stagg to remark, "It looked as though Sherman had just marched through it. That private car proved to be a joke on us."[100]

Back on the Midway, Harper and Stagg eagerly embraced the growing enthusiasm for football among the University of Chicago's student body. Reflecting on his recent pilgrimage, Stagg offered his thoughts on the merits of intercollegiate football in a letter to his friend and mentor Walter Camp: "Football has done a great deal toward arousing college spirit where little or none existed, so we feel it has been of special value in our university life. In fact, our athletics have done more to create a college spirit than all the rest of the student organizations."[101]

Camp employed Stagg's words in defense of the game as he addressed the mounting criticism of football's dangers. The men soon emerged as two of the game's most vocal and influential champions of reform.

Stagg planned to return to the West for a mid-winter clash with Pacific Coast teams in 1896, but financial constraints prohibited the football squad from making the journey. Receipts from the Maroons' Thanksgiving Day game were not sufficient to fund a cross-country trip, and Stagg refused to borrow money or request that the university finance football travel expenses.[102]

*Chapter 6*

# FOOTBALL FIRSTS

I n February 1896, the forerunner of the Big Ten, the Western Conference, was founded by Alonzo Stagg and representatives from the Universities of Illinois, Michigan, Minnesota and Wisconsin, as well as Northwestern and Purdue.[103] The conference would eventually add Indiana (1900), Iowa (1900) and Ohio State (1913).[104] The University of Chicago remained a member of the conference for forty-four years.[105]

Rivalries naturally grew from the establishment of a conference of schools. Harper and Stagg seized the opportunity to leverage benefits to Chicago's football program by continuing to rally students in support of the team. And as the university began to graduate its first classes, they encouraged alumni to return to campus to root for Maroon football.

The two men also recognized an opportunity to promote civic support for the team as it established an identity on the Midway. Horace Butterworth, manager of Maroon athletics, identified two strategic target groups within the community: the "society element" and the public. Butterworth then helped to advance Harper and Stagg's vision through strategic scheduling of football games, reasoning "early season victories promoted attendance and enthusiasm for the later season contests."[106]

As the Maroons gained a following, local journalists lobbied for a rivalry game on the order of Harvard-Yale in the East; Stagg and company delivered with a late-season Chicago-Michigan contest. Scheduling the annual meeting scored on two fronts: it created a school tradition, and it provided a high-profile venue for Chicago's elite to see and be seen. For over a decade, Chicago played Michigan at the end of the season, typically on Thanksgiving Day, in front of capacity crowds.

Alonzo Stagg identified a third constituency of support for Chicago football: "college people"—individuals who had attended other schools and whose loyalty could be transferred to Chicago. He estimated fifty thousand people to make up this group.[107] The university promoted the Maroons to each contingent of fans—both inside and outside the Midway campus—and to the increasingly interested local press.

Historian Robin Lester declared the "rise of the spectator" at the University of Chicago the most significant development of the era in college athletics.[108] As football was introduced in Chicago's secondary schools in the mid- to late 1890s, public interest began to grow, but it is widely accepted that Alonzo Stagg and William Rainey Harper deserve credit for growing enthusiasm for football in Chicago during the period. From 1896 to 1905, the University of Chicago played almost 90 percent of its games at home, to the delight of Maroon faithful.[109] And Chicago's renown translated to gains for its opponents as well—in the early days of the Western Conference, member schools earned half of their season's income in games against Chicago.[110]

In their final contest of the 1896 season, the Maroons met Michigan at the new Chicago Coliseum—the first football game to be played in the indoor arena south of the Midway campus. Just months before, the venue had opened with Buffalo Bill's Wild West Show and had hosted the Democratic National Convention, where William Jennings Bryan delivered his famous "Cross of Gold" speech. To prepare the stadium for the football game, crews removed the floor, leaving a natural clay playing surface, which they watered and packed down with a steamroller. Teams of construction workers also erected stands on the sides and at each end of the field, increasing the capacity to fourteen thousand seats. In the days leading up to the Chicago-Michigan game, the *Chicago Tribune* predicted a "Shakespearean drama" to play out on the indoor gridiron, with a cacophony of tin horns and cheering crowds reverberating through the Coliseum. The stadium was indeed loud, as the crowd's cheering "echoed about so that the noise united into one continuous roar without rhyme or reason."[111] While spectators expressed dissatisfaction with the noise, the athletes complained of the stadium's slippery playing surface. Although the conditions inside the Coliseum left both participants and patrons wanting, the stadium did protect those assembled from the driving rain that fell on the city throughout the afternoon. And when the Chicago sky darkened in the downpour, the building's engineers turned on the interior electric lights—the innovation of modern technology allowing play to continue.[112]

Michigan relied heavily on the run, and its offense struggled to gain traction sufficient to advance the ball. Early in the first half, Chicago forced the Wolverines to punt from their own one-yard line. Maroon right end Ralph Hamill rushed through Michigan's line just as James Hogg received the ball to kick. From Hogg's toe, the ball ricocheted off Hamill's chest and into the stands behind the goal line. Players scrambled after the loose ball as fans fell over their seats trying to avoid the oncoming rush. Reaching the football as it landed in the aisle, the Wolverine kicker jumped on the bouncing pigskin for a Chicago safety. The score remained 2–0 for the next thirty minutes as the two sides continued their defensive battle, allowing only short gains with no scores.

Midway through the second half, after a series of long punts that pinned the Wolverines deep in their own territory, Chicago's Clarence Herschberger received the ball at the forty-five-yard line and executed what Michigan captain Giovanni Villa later called "a drop kick that has never been equaled."[113] Chicago allowed a late Wolverine touchdown but prevailed by a 7–6 margin.

The Thanksgiving Day victory over Michigan capped Chicago's 15-2-1 season, during which time the Maroons traveled beyond the Windy City's confines only twice.

During this period, Stagg also seized the opportunity to promote the game and its play at other institutions while supporting his former pupils. In 1896, Chicago quarterback Frank Hering was hired by the University of Notre Dame as a student-coach. Hering brought what he had learned from Stagg to South Bend as he grew the small Catholic school's nascent football program. Stagg helped Hering cultivate interest and support for Notre Dame football by agreeing to bring his increasingly popular Maroons to play Hering's eleven in South Bend. The two teams met at the Indiana campus three times between 1896 and 1899.[114]

Much like his teacher, Hering displayed skills as an innovator. In the schools' November 6, 1897 contest, Stagg's disciple scripted a play that took the Maroons "entirely unawares" and resulted in college football history.

Throughout the opening minutes of the game, the two teams traded possessions without scoring, due in large measure to fumbles and penalties. Midway through the first half, Notre Dame recovered a Chicago fumble and, on its first snap, attempted an end play that resulted in a loss. On the following play, Notre Dame fullback Mike Daly dropped back and kicked the ball from the thirty-five-yard line using the "Princeton place-kick method."[115] This marked the first time a non-eastern team employed a place kick from scrimmage to score a field goal.[116]

The 5-point field goal was Notre Dame's only score. Chicago righted its ship and reached the end zone six times, successfully adding 2-point kicks after five of the touchdowns for a 34–5 victory.[117] Daly's historic kick, however, inspired Notre Dame instructor Michael McGrisken to pen the following in his "Seventh Latin" class the Monday following the game:

*Mike Daly's Kick*

*Chicago's pride came down a peg*
*At that outrageous mystery;*
*How Daly ever kept his leg*
*When his kick went down to history.*

*He felt his calf. There was a cheer*
*That boded much security.*
*As Daly kicked, and sent the sphere*
*Revolving through futurity.*

*Up through the azure hurled,*
*And, lo, another satellite,*
*Revolving 'round the world.*[118]

When Chicago met Michigan at the Coliseum on Thanksgiving Day 1897, Herschberger again was the hero. Borrowing from the Hering playbook, Stagg called on Herschberger to attempt the Princeton place kick field goal, which the Peoria native successfully executed three times. He also added a kick after Billy Gardner's thirty-three-yard touchdown run. In all, Herschberger was responsible for 17 Chicago points in his team's 21–12 defeat of the Wolverines.[119]

As the popularity of college football spread throughout the Midwest, Alonzo Stagg continued innovating. In 1896, he began using wind sprints during practice to improve his players' endurance. Stagg, a daily runner, reasoned that his men would often line up against bigger opponents, but they would make up for any size deficits with superior conditioning. Also in 1896, Stagg originated the short punt formation using Herschberger to receive a direct pass from center, five to six yards behind line of scrimmage, with the quarterback serving as a blocking back.[120]

In 1897, Stagg implemented line shifts in formations. In 1898, he expanded his use of the lateral pass into plays from scrimmage: an end, after receiving the ball from the quarterback, ran across the field behind the line and tossed the ball with a "basketball toss" to the halfback circling back behind the blockers.[121]

President Harper also contributed to the game's transformation during the era. In 1897, he requested the addition of a sideline "bulletin board" at Marshall Field to allow spectators to see and understand what was happening.[122] Harper's request was granted. Adjacent to the field, a scorekeeper used a large blackboard and chalk to tell the game's story on football's earliest scoreboard.[123]

Alonzo Stagg introduced the man-in-motion in 1899.[124] He used it in conjunction with the T-formation, putting a player in motion behind the offensive line. Stagg's former players who entered coaching widely disseminated the man-in-motion and his other contributions to football's strategies by implementing them at their own institutions.[125]

Even science found a role in the evolution of football in the late nineteenth century, thanks to the University of Chicago's renowned physicist Dr. A.A. Michaelson. During the Maroons' October 30, 1897 game at Illinois, Clarence Herschberger injured his foot. When his squad returned to the Midway, Stagg sent the Maroon captain to the university's Ryerson Physical Laboratory, where the physics department chairman used a Röntgen ray to view the bones of Herschberger's injured foot. The first diagnostic use of an X-ray on a football player revealed no break, and after a week of rest, Herschberger was cleared to play.[126] Notwithstanding the significance of his contribution to the field of sports medicine, Michaelson's work with the Maroon star was far from his magnum opus. Ten years after his look into Clarence Herschberger's foot, the University of Chicago professor received the 1907 Nobel Prize in Physics for his work with "optical precision instruments and the spectroscopic and metrological investigations carried out with their aid," distinguishing himself as the first American scientist to receive the prize.[127]

As college football advanced in the West, power brokers in the East presided over the evolution of intercollegiate sports press coverage. William Randolph Hearst's circulation duel with Joseph Pulitzer for dominance in New York's news business led Hearst to develop sports journalism, predicting it would lead to an increase in his readership. Within a few years, the "sporting page" had displaced the society page as the permanent home for collegiate sports reporting in newspapers from coast to coast. During this emergence of sports journalism, Stagg and his Maroons gave writers at the Windy City newspapers plenty of material to fill their columns, which journalists did enthusiastically.[128] By the early twentieth century, the press's affection for University of Chicago football extended to the other schools in the conference. In November 1902, the Chicago Press Club hosted what became the first annual Gridiron Fest, a banquet that brought together coaches, team managers and players from each of the Western Conference schools with football officials and members of the press.[129] Its stated goal was to make the conference representatives better acquainted with local newspapermen, and the outcome was "bonhomie and goodwill [that] made enough touchdowns to last until another gridiron season arrived."[130]

*Chapter 7*

# FATHERHOOD AND THE OLYMPIC GAMES

**S**tella and Alonzo welcomed their first child, Amos Alonzo Stagg Jr., on April 11, 1899. The younger Stagg's childhood was steeped in Chicago football, as he learned the game by observing his father's coaching and his mother's meticulous note taking. He joined his father on the sidelines of practice, and he studied his mother's charts and diagrams on the living room floor. In an interview many years later, he was asked about growing up as a son of the legendary coach. The younger Stagg recalled attending his first football game—the epic 1905 contest between Chicago and the University of Michigan. He spoke of playing quarterback for his father at Chicago and sharing the sidelines with "Mr. Stagg" at Susquehanna University.

But "my greatest appreciation of my father," Alonzo Jr. said, "is that he saved my life."

"When I was seven months old," Stagg explained, "I came down with diphtheria. This was before vaccines, antidotes, penicillin, and sulfa drugs to fight it. The only thing was care and the good fortune of a person with enough stamina to live through it. My father for 26 hours picked me up and walked me. Every time my face turned black with croup, he turned me over and spanked me. Of course, it brought out great anger in me, and I would redden up and fight it. But each time, I managed to get my breath again. Some way or another, this great inborn fight came out and I lived through it. I was one person probably marked for death, but it didn't happen because of my father."[131]

In the summer of 1900, Stagg prepared to travel to Paris with a team of University of Chicago runners competing in the Olympic Games. As he readied to leave for his extended trip, Stagg did so "with an extra load on his mind" as he thought of his son's narrow escape from death.[132] Recognizing the dangers of transatlantic travel and the possibility of not returning home to his family, the young father penned a letter to his fourteen-month-old son shortly before he and his team departed on their five-week journey:

*June 23, 1900*

*To my Son, Amos Alonzo Stagg, Jr.:*
*You are only a little fellow now—a trifle over fourteen months old; but I have loved you so dearly since you came, that it has been on my mind to write you a letter, in the event of my being taken away—at any time before I have a chance to tell you the many things which you need to know.*

*Your father wants his boy to love, protect and care for his mother, giving to her the same kind measure of love and devotion which she has given to you. Second, your father wants his boy to be sincere, honest and upright. Be your true self always. Hate dishonesty and trickery no matter how big and how great the thing desired may be. Third, your father wants you to have a proper independence of thought, feeling and action. Think matters out for yourself always where it relates to your own conduct and act honestly afterwards.*

*Fourth, your father wants you to be an American in democracy. Treat everybody with courtesy and as your equal until he proves his untrustworthiness to be so treated. The man and the soul are what counts— not family and not appearance. Fifth, your father wants you to "abhor evil." No curiosity, no imagination, no conversation, no story, no reading which suggests impurity of life is worthy of your thought or attention. I beg you never to yield for an instant but turn thought to something good and helpful.*

*Sixth, train yourself to be master of yourself; of your thought and imagination, temper, passion, appetite and of your body. Hold all absolutely under your will. Allow no thought nor imagination, passion, nor appetite to injure your mind or body. Hold all absolutely under your will. Your father has never used intoxicating liquors, nor tobacco, nor profane language and he wants his boy to be like him in this regard.*

*Seventh, your father wants his boy enthusiastic and earnest in all of his interests—his sports, his studies, his work; and he wants him always to keep an active, actual participation in each so long as he lives. It is my judgment that one's life is richest, most healthy and most successful when lived out on such a basis. Eighth, your father wants his son to love God as he is revealed to him; which after all will be the revelation of all that I have said and left unsaid of good to you, my precious boy.*

*Affectionately,*
*Your Father*[133]

Stagg and his squad set sail from New York to London, and after arriving safely, the athletes competed in the weeklong English championships. From London, Stagg and company traveled to Paris for the opening of the Olympics on July 7.[134] There, the men of Chicago joined track and field stars from Georgetown, Penn, Princeton, Syracuse and Yale on the world stage.[135] The team of U.S. runners dominated their competitors, winning eighteen of twenty-one Olympic events.[136]

Alonzo Stagg Sr. and the Olympic champions returned home unscathed, having borne witness to history: the last Olympic Games of the century were the first to include female athletes.[137] Notwithstanding the historic significance of women's participation, the 1900 Paris games were rife with confusion and controversy. Under the auspices of the Exposition Universelle Internationale de 1900 a Paris, the contests stretched from May through October with no opening or closing ceremonies. And in violation of agreed-upon terms, the hosts scheduled competitions on Sundays, a highly unorthodox practice in the United States at the time. The games also hold the distinction of including such nontraditional Olympic events as balloon racing, basque pelota, cannon shooting, cricket, croquet and live pigeon shooting—most of which did not appear in future games.[138]

Four years later, Stagg joined the city of Chicago as it hosted the first Olympics held in the United States.[139] Stagg went on to serve as a member of the American Olympic Games Committee from 1906 to 1932, and at the 1924 Paris games, he also coached the four-hundred-meter and eight-hundred-meter runners.[140] During an era when the growth of intercollegiate football was synonymous with the names Stagg and Chicago, the Grand Old Man simultaneously imprinted his mark on the sport of track with three decades of service in promoting it at home and abroad.

As a new century dawned, football continued to evolve, and Alonzo Stagg continued to drive its evolution.

In 1900, he developed what came to be known as the "whoa-back" formation, where both ends stood in the backfield with one end behind the fullback as a pusher when the fullback or halfbacks bucked. The other end stood in front of the fullback and shifted to the right or left, according to the play call. The Maroons executed the play to perfection against Michigan on November 29, as the pusher catapulted fullback Ernie Perkins through for multiple gains, despite giving up an average of ten pounds per man to the Wolverines.[141] Perkins's three touchdowns secured Chicago's 15–6 victory and made him the talk of the Midway throughout the holiday season. (All plays pulling linemen into the backfield became illegal with a rule change in 1910 that required seven men to remain on the offensive line of scrimmage.)[142]

In 1901, Stagg's Maroons were the first to practice under lights and were the first to use a white painted ball in practice[143]—innovations inspired by the coach's desire to continue his team's preparation after dark.

The indefatigable Stagg guided football into a new era, but vestiges of its rugby roots remained with the gridiron game. At the turn of the twentieth century, football gained notoriety for the number of injuries and deaths suffered by players on high school, college and club teams. In Chicago alone, at least three players died in the fall of 1900 from injuries they sustained in games.[144] President Theodore Roosevelt intervened and demanded change in the play of college football. The College Football Rules Committee was established, and in 1904, Alonzo Stagg joined the committee as its first non-eastern representative.[145]

While Stagg continued his work at home and abroad, a trailblazer 235 miles to the east was making his mark on the game. Fielding Yost arrived in Ann Arbor in 1901 after coaching at Stanford for one year. Yost brought an entirely new brand of football to Michigan—one that emphasized speed. So frequent were Yost's admonitions for his team to "hurry up" that the call became his nickname.

Beginning his first season, Yost instructed his quarterback, Harrison "Boss" Weeks, to call the next play while the team was getting up from the last play. As the linemen jumped into position, Weeks would call another signal, but with the first number as the starting signal, the center would immediately snap the ball. This strategy often caught the opposing team off guard. When its opponents learned Michigan's tactics and charged on the first signal, Yost would call for the center to delay the snap and cause the defense to jump offsides, resulting in a penalty giving the Wolverines a first down and gain of five yards.[146]

"Hurry Up" Yost's first Wolverine squad went 11-0, including a 15–6 season finale win against Chicago. Over the next three seasons, Michigan remained undefeated, its 29-game winning streak interrupted by a 6–6 tie against Minnesota on Halloween 1903. From 1901 to 1904, Michigan scored an astonishing 2,326 points and allowed only 40, 12 of which were scored by Chicago.[147]

*\*\**

In July 1903, Alonzo Stagg added long-distance walking to his list of athletic pursuits as he happily traded cradling a football for carrying his newborn daughter, Ruth. The Staggs' daughter made her debut on the sidelines of Maroons' practice within a few months of her birth. By her third birthday, she was also a regular participant at "Baby Day on the Midway," an annual party hosted by the University of Chicago's dean of women.[148]

## Chapter 8

# THE ENGINE DRIVING PROGRESS

**B**etween 1903 and 1905, Alonzo Stagg scheduled twenty-eight games at home and five away. Revenues earned by the Maroon football team covered its expenses and provided the necessary financing for other sports and activities in the Department of Physical Culture and Athletics at the University of Chicago.[149]

The Maroons played host to the University of Texas in early November 1904. Among the spectators at the game were Michigan's head coach and team captain. Coach Yost and Willie Heston arrived without fanfare and escaped notice as they reached their seats atop the east stands. Once spotted by Maroon fans, however, the pair became the target of good-natured ribbing.[150]

"Hey, Coach! Take a look at those Texas Longhorns. You'll be in their shoes next Saturday."

Yost smiled as he looked down on the field where the Chicago backs were tearing through the Texas defense. "Those cattle are no wolverines," he responded.

In the lead-up to Michigan's game with Wisconsin the week before, Yost had fired a shot across Chicago's bow with the local press: "Wisconsin always plays us a hard game. They are the hardest team in the West to beat, much harder than Chicago. We have never had a great deal of trouble beating Chicago."[151]

As the first half of the Chicago-Texas game drew to a close, members of the Maroon-friendly press joined in the fun.

"This just in from Ann Arbor. Drake scores twice on Michigan," the public-address announcer relayed to the Chicago crowd. As the Maroon faithful cheered, Yost's expression turned serious. The head Wolverine had left his squad in what he assumed were the capable hands of assistant coach King Cole while he and Heston conducted their reconnaissance on the Midway.

At the announcement, taunts rained down on the Michigan duo.

"Well, what do you think of that?" Yost declared. "When the cat is away the mice will play. We should have known enough to stay at home, eh, Heston?'"

In truth, Drake kicked only one field goal in the 36–4 Wolverine victory— but that hardly mattered to the scores of Chicagoans delighting in the angst of their arch-nemesis Yost.[152]

As Michigan sealed its ninth win of the season, Chicago thoroughly dismantled the Texas defense and held the Longhorn offense scoreless in a 68–0 rout to secure its ninth victory. After witnessing the impressive display, both Yost and Heston declared their growing respect for the Maroon squad.[153]

***

Stagg was the face of the university, and the Chicago public eagerly consumed news of him and his gridiron boys.[154] The appearance of two-year-old Alonzo Stagg Jr. and his father on the sidelines of Marshall Field marked the "official" beginning of the 1902 Maroon football season, and that same year, a journalist at the *Chicago Chronicle* declared that the head football coach was "better known than anyone connected with University of Chicago" (other than perhaps John D. Rockefeller).

By 1905, Stagg was the best-known figure in intercollegiate athletics west of the Appalachians, and Walter Camp had christened him "dean" of western football.[155]

Though barely forty years old, Alonzo Stagg became known as the Grand Old Man of Football. His players, however, called him simply "Mr. Stagg."

As Chicago football's prominence grew, so did advances in the game—due in large measure to Stagg's acumen. He pushed for innovation as a tactician-coach with a long-term view of the sport and its benefits. He continued to devise plays that helped his often undersized athletes catch opposing teams off guard.

One such innovation was the shift formation, about which Stagg said, "At the beginning of the century, I was shifting linemen quickly from one side to the other for a quick attack, and in 1904 I sometimes used a backfield shift synchronously."[156]

Another Stagg innovation, once sanctioned by the Rules Committee, would revolutionize the game of college football.

## Chapter 9

# ENDING THE STREAK

Coach Stagg's Maroons hosted the University of Michigan on Thanksgiving Day 1905 for the final game of the season. Coming into the fourteenth gridiron match-up between the midwestern foes, Michigan held a 9-4 series lead over Chicago.[157]

The men of Ann Arbor rode into Chicago on a run of fifty-six games without a loss, spanning nearly five years.[158] Their last defeat came on October 29, 1900, against Chicago, in the Wolverines' final season under coach Biff Lea.[159] Through the first twelve games of the '05 season, Michigan scored a staggering 495 points while holding its opponents scoreless. The Maroons entered the final game with a 10-0 record, having given up only 5 points all season: a 16–5 win over Indiana on October 14.[160]

In what would rightly be called the first "Game of the Century," the November 30 contest showcased an epic battle between Fielding Yost's "point a minute" team and the original Monsters of the Midway for the championship of the West—a purely symbolic prize for the best collegiate team west of Pennsylvania.[161] The Wolverines fielded three All-Americas and four who were named to the All-Western team,[162] including Tom Hammond, a Hyde Park High School standout coveted by both Yost and Stagg.[163] Chicago boasted four All-Americas and eight All-Western selections, including All-time All-America quarterback Walter Eckersall and future College Football Hall of Fame coach Hugo Bezdek.

Stagg and the Maroons worked overtime to prepare for the match-up with Michigan. Stagg held secret nighttime practices by electric lights inside a specially constructed, twelve-foot-high "stockade," and as the team practiced, a corps of watchmen patrolled the only building with a view of the field.[164] The Grand Old Man had witnessed his team fall to the Wolverines each of the previous four seasons, and he was determined to prevent a fifth loss.

Snowfall and temperatures hovering around ten degrees above zero could not dampen the enthusiasm among the Maroon and Wolverine faithful entering the stands at Marshall Field. A capacity crowd of over twenty-seven thousand braved the elements to witness the contest. In the two weeks prior to the game, over fifty thousand requests for tickets flooded the athletic offices in Chicago. Widespread scalping resulted as fans of both teams scrambled to find seats. A local newspaper reported "ticket scalping…on the Michigan-Chicago game is a record-breaker for a sporting event in Chicago." Chief among the grifters were Chicago students who received special consideration to purchase tickets early for prime location seats.[165]

Walter Camp joined the spectators, presumably scouting for his All-America team and no doubt eager to observe the playbook of Lonnie Stagg, whose Maroons had bested his Stanford team a decade earlier. In 1889, Camp had selected the Maroons' head coach to his first All-America team following a successful season at left end for Yale. In 1905, Chicago's quarterback, Walter Eckersall, was the object of Camp's interest.[166]

Chicago native Eckersall spent his formative years watching Stagg's Maroons, and his love for the game was born. As he later told an interviewer for the *Chicago American*, "We little fellows couldn't buy footballs, but we caught the spirit of the game from watching Stagg's players racing around in practice and in real games. I guess we all dreamed of becoming football heroes."[167] During his impressive career at nearby Hyde Park High School, Eckersall garnered the interest of college football coaches from the Midwest to the East. Stagg and Yost were chief among rivals recruiting the star and his teammate Tom Hammond. Confident in Eckersall's decision to play for his hometown team, Stagg preemptively announced in the fall of 1902 that he had secured Eckersall's commitment to Chicago for the following year. Yost, however, was unwilling to wave the white flag, and Michigan pressed harder in its pursuit of Eckersall, through what Yost's competitors termed "rare inducements" offered by "secret embassies."[168]

Eckersall remained uncommitted into the summer of 1903. As the start of the fall semester approached, Stagg's patience waned. He refused to lose the local star to the rival Wolverines. When Stagg learned that Eckersall was preparing to travel from his home to the University of Michigan, he took matters into his own hands.

The Maroon head man met Eckersall at Chicago's Englewood train station, and after a brief but persuasive pitch, Stagg facilitated the young man's commitment to the University of Chicago by removing him from the platform where he waited to board a train to Ann Arbor.[169] (Today's NCAA would no doubt frown upon Fielding Yost's and Alonzo Stagg's behaviors, but with collegiate football still in its infancy, strict guidelines for recruiting practices were yet to be established and enforced.)

The Chicago-Michigan game did not disappoint for Coach Camp and the throng of witnesses; it showcased the machine-like skill of the two teams' defenses—and the kicking prowess of its two punters. In the first half, Chicago's Eckersall punted twelve times and Michigan's John Garrels ten. During one Eckersall punt early in the first half, Michigan's left tackle, Joe Curtis, charged through the line in an attempt to block the kick. Following the play, Eckersall remained motionless on the ground for nearly two minutes before regaining consciousness. The officials ejected Curtis for rough play, and Michigan lost a leading scorer and tackler for the rest of the game.

The Maize and Blue allowed the Maroons to cross midfield only three times in the first half, and Michigan crossed into Chicago territory only once.[170]

University of Chicago president Harper, terminally ill with cancer, was unable to attend the game in person and instead relied on his wife and son Paul for the game's play-by-play. The younger Harper watched the game from the window of his Hitchcock Hall room and described the events to his father by telephone. So agitated was Dr. Harper by the scoreless game that at halftime he dispatched language professor Elizabeth Wallace (his nurse for the day) to the locker room to deliver to Stagg a message: "The boys must win this game." Professor Wallace arrived at the locker room to find the team had already taken the field for the second half. Before they left, however, Stagg had conveyed his own message to the players, pleading with them to win for the sake of the dying president.[171]

Twenty-three years later, Knute Rockne would famously employ a similar strategy to rally his Fighting Irish to upset a previously undefeated Army team.[172] And in 1940, Rockne's "Win one for the Gipper" speech was immortalized in *Knute Rockne, All American*, featuring Amos Alonzo Stagg in a cameo role as himself.[173]

Behind the leadership of their quarterback, the Maroons opened the second half with renewed fire, as Eckersall led his team in a game-changing drive. A long Michigan punt and a Chicago penalty left the Maroons pinned deep in their own territory. Eckersall dropped back to his own end zone to punt the ball and instead tucked it and ran around the left end for a twenty-

COLLEGE FOOTBALL'S MAN IN MOTION

yard gain. The Maroons continued their march down the field but were ultimately held on fourth down. Eckersall booted the ball from his own forty-five-yard line into the Wolverines' end zone. Michigan's Dennison "Denny" Clark fielded the kick and began to run from the shadow of his goalpost. He dodged a tackle and crossed the goal line, but Chicago's Art Badenoch and Mark Catlin drove him back into the end zone and tackled him for a safety. The defensive stalemate continued, and as the game neared its end, Michigan's Garrels faked a punt and dashed down the sideline. Chicago's utility man Eckersall tackled the Wolverine punter, preventing a touchdown and preserving the win for the Maroons. Clark's safety marked the game's only score, and the game marked the first collegiate defeat experienced by any of the men in a Michigan uniform.[174]

As the Maroons ran victorious off the field, Eckersall maneuvered through the crowd to find his head coach. "Mr. Stagg!" Eckersall greeted the Old Man with a vigorous embrace.

"Walter, you son of a gun. It's a good thing I grabbed you off that train to Ann Arbor!"

An exuberant Chicago crowd launched into a campus-wide celebration. Students flooded Marshall Field and hoisted Captain Catlin and the rest of the team on their shoulders. As Stagg attempted to slip away quietly from the euphoria, a group of students spotted him and lifted him from his feet; they circled the field before depositing the Grand Old Man along with his players at Bartlett Gymnasium, where the revelry continued. Inside the gym, Professor Oliver Thatcher embraced Stagg, and the two danced "a cross between a double shuffle and a cakewalk" before Frank Bell, another Maroon booster, cut in and continued the dance with the uncharacteristically gregarious coach.[175]

Stagg made his way across the gym to a stocky figure sitting alone on the bench. "Beautiful, Bezdek—beautiful!" exclaimed the coach as he embraced the grimy fullback. Bezdek grinned with joy at the unexpected display of emotion.[176]

Outside the gym, a group of 2,500 students and alumni led by the university band marched on President Harper's house to serenade him with the alma mater.[177] As the night wore on, students pilfered wood from several Hyde Park garden fences and outhouses to fuel a huge bonfire that was accompanied by "a nightshirt parade and war dance."[178]

In keeping with tradition, the Maroon players broke training with a Thanksgiving dinner in Hitchcock Hall. And as a hat tip to their effort against the Wolverines, Stagg lifted his long-standing ban on inviting co-eds to the banquet.[179] "You have all earned it," he declared as he looked out over the room filled with smiling faces. "The boys are bruised and sore, but we cleaned 'em up for you," said Stagg, addressing the ladies in the crowd.

Meanwhile in Ann Arbor, the weight of the game-turning play sat heavy on the shoulders of Denny Clark. "My error [in picking up the ball and trying to run it out from behind the goal posts, where it had rolled on a kick by Eckersall] was flagrant and the worst possible," Clark said in an interview with a local reporter. With tears welling in his eyes, he continued, "My misplay was inexcusable, in view of the fact that I had been coached against this very thing. I cannot say how sorry I am. Mr. Yost and all the boys have treated me handsomely and I appreciate their consideration."[180]

Two days after the historic Western Conference battle, another notable contest played out in the East. The Midshipmen of the U.S. Naval Academy and the Cadets of the U.S. Military Academy met in Princeton, New Jersey, for the eleventh installment of their storied rivalry.[181] President Roosevelt's attendance, while customary for the commander-in-chief, placed the teams' play under increased scrutiny by virtue of his recent denunciation of the game's brutality. Both sides played "gentlemanly football," with the exception of West Point's left guard Henry Weeks, who was ejected for "roughing" a Navy player. Officials were forced to call the game due to darkness with four minutes left to play in the second half, resulting in a 6–6 tie—a first for the series.[182]

Cries for changes in the game's play notwithstanding, Maroon football helped Chicago strengthen the bond among its students, as Harper and Stagg hoped it would.[183] The university had been established after the discontinuation of compulsory chapel in most American universities, leaving it, like so many other institutions, without a school-wide gathering point.[184] Harper and Stagg understood the challenge of creating campus unity in a secular, co-educational environment; they developed the Department of Athletics and Physical Education to promote a well-rounded education for Chicago's students, knowing that those students would also find common cause in cheering on the Maroons in the stands around Marshall Field. The victory over Michigan and the ensuing revelry further unified Chicago students with a shared enthusiasm that transcended their otherwise disparate academic interests.[185]

## Chapter 10

# THE FORWARD PASS
# AND A CHAMPIONSHIP RUN

**A**s an outcry over the brutality of the game rained down on football, President Roosevelt became the leading voice in a chorus demanding reform. The *Chicago Tribune* reported that during the 1905 season, 18 players died and another 159 sustained serious injuries. Midway through the season, President Roosevelt summoned representatives from Yale, Harvard and Princeton to the White House and instructed them to remove the "foul play" from the sport in order for it to continue. Representatives of thirteen eastern schools met on December 9 and agreed to initial reforms. Then, in a December 28 meeting, representatives from sixty-two schools organized the Intercollegiate Athletic Association of the United States to "assist in the formation of sound requirements for intercollegiate athletics, particularly football."[186]

In January 1906, the sixty-two-member Football Rules Committee, led by West Point's Captain Palmer Pierce, merged with Walter Camp's self-selected American Football Rules Committee to form the American Intercollegiate Football Rules Committee.[187] In 1910, the group changed its name to the National Collegiate Athletic Association (NCAA).[188]

Out of this inaugural meeting on January 12, 1906, came the legalization of the forward pass—the most consequential advance in the game since the introductions of scrimmage and the system of downs.[189]

The committee's endorsement of the forward pass marked a turning away from the game's reliance on running formations featuring the "mass attack of brute force"[190] that resembled the colliding of beasts on the plains of the

Serengeti. Football play in its first half century was akin to ground warfare without firearms. The ubiquitous "flying wedge," first used by Harvard and then adopted throughout college football, was in fact developed by Lorin Deland based on the principles of warfare. "My 'Momentum Play,'" Deland explained to Walter Camp, "was nothing more or less than the application to football of some of Napoleon's methods for turning the enemy's flank."[191]

Several men are credited with introducing the forward pass to football, including its most enthusiastic proponents, Rules Committee members Walter Camp, John Heisman and Alonzo Stagg. History records the first use of the forward pass in a game during the 1876 contest between Yale and Princeton. According to *Athletics at Princeton: A History* (1900), Walter Camp, as he was being tackled, "threw the ball forward to Oliver Thompson, who ran for a touchdown."[192] Princeton cried foul on the play, and the referee tossed a coin to determine how to rule. The coin landed in Yale's favor, and the play stood.

The next mention of the forward pass's use came in 1895, during the North Carolina–Georgia game. John Heisman, then head coach at Auburn, was standing near the Carolina backfield as the Tar Heels lined up in punt formation. Dodging the Bulldog rush at his goal line, the Carolina fullback, instead of kicking, threw the ball to the left halfback, who ran seventy yards for a touchdown. Georgia head coach Glenn "Pop" Warner protested the illegal pass, but a referee who did not see the pass allowed the play and the winning touchdown to stand.[193] Heisman, a vocal opponent of mass formations and their resulting injuries, wondered if he had witnessed the answer to the flying wedge. He began a campaign to permit the forward pass "as a means of opening up both the attack and the defense."[194]

As the addition of the forward pass made more options available, coaches' playbooks began to include open, quick-strike plays, increasing the game's speed—along with spectators' enjoyment. In 1906, Stagg's repertoire contained sixty-four pass plays, including the first recorded use of a flanker in conjunction with the forward pass.[195] Immediately after Chicago's thirty-nine-point shutout of Purdue on October 20, several officials and coaches commented on the prominently featured forward pass. Coach Jimmy Sheldon of Indiana watched the game from the sidelines and offered a cautiously optimistic outlook on the new rules, declaring, "It is still early, but I think much will be made of the forward pass."[196]

In 1908, Stagg incorporated a fake pass and developed the idea of the run-pass option. That same year, he devised a double pass—between a halfback and end—and established the principle of the Statue of Liberty play. By 1910, Stagg was using a flanker in motion to run in and block the defensive end.[197]

At the same time the forward pass became legal, kicking took on a more prominent role. In the eleven games played on November 10, 1906, between college and university teams (i.e., games not including non-majors), twenty-one touchdowns and eight field goals were scored. In two of the contests, kicks decided the game's outcome. This ratio of approximately two and a half touchdowns to one field goal represented a marked decrease in the proportion of scoring from touchdowns compared to the nine seasons since the field goal's inception. The change prompted one sportswriter to observe, "The college game is now literally 'football' and no longer 'pushball,' 'rushball,' or 'slugball.'"[198]

In his last collegiate game, a 38–5 Maroon victory over Nebraska on November 24, 1906, Walter Eckersall kicked five field goals, a feat he first accomplished a year earlier against Illinois. This single-game record number of field goals stood for seventy-eight years.[199]

Stagg's Maroons ended the shortened 1906 season with a 4-1 record, outscoring their opponents 175–17.[200] Quarterback Wally Steffen led the Maroons to a 63–0 rout of Illinois on November 17, as the team rebounded from its only loss—a 4–2 defeat by Minnesota on November 10.[201] Steffen scored five of Chicago's ten touchdowns, with Pat Page, John Schommer and Walter Eckersall also reaching the end zone against the Illini.

In the fall of 1905, Chicago native Steffen enrolled at the university and joined the Maroon gridiron squad after more than a year of being pursued by the University of Wisconsin. Steffen's matriculation at Chicago followed "the most strenuous 'rushing' probably ever given a 'prep' school athlete in the west"—exceeding even the overtures made to Walter Eckersall. But Steffen's attendance at Chicago did not deter Wisconsin head coach Philip King and captain Edward Vanderboom from traveling to the Midway in early October to visit with the highly coveted athlete. The Badger duo escorted Steffen to Madison, where he attended practice, fulfilling an earlier promise "to see what they had."[202] Steffen returned to Chicago after a three-day sojourn, declaring his embarrassment over the affair, saying, "I made the trip to Wisconsin entirely against my will. For a month I endeavored in every way to avoid going to Madison as a guest, but the pressure became so strong that I could not resist. I told them before I went that I could not enter Wisconsin under any circumstances, and an hour after my arrival I told them that I would not remain. They told me that if I once saw Madison I would never return to Chicago. I was ashamed to make the trip.…I like Chicago…and I intend to stick here until I get my degree."[203] Steffen admitted he secretly hoped "to get up there and get back before anyone would know about it."[204] Upon Steffen's return to the Midway, Stagg responded with a judicious willingness to pardon the young man's actions, stating that "the athletic department would take 'no official notice' of Steffen's confused behavior."[205]

When the University of Chicago became the first in the nation to award letters to athletes in 1906, Stagg named Maroon standout Steffen to the inaugural class of the letterman's club he called the "Order of the C."[206]

In the years that followed, alumni members of the "C Club" returned to Chicago for the annual banquet each spring as new inductees received their letters. The men gathered in Bartlett Gymnasium's trophy room, where they each sang "The Song of the 'C'" to Stagg. According to custom, letter winners were required to sing the members-only song to their coach in order to receive their "C"[207]—a lesson learned the hard way by an All-America fullback years later when he failed to sing the song to his coach and lost his opportunity to receive his "C" button.[208]

In 1907, the Maroons again marched through their Western Conference foes with ease. In preparation for the season finale on November 23, Stagg drilled his undefeated squad on a new play he designed for the matchup with Pop Warner's Carlisle Indians. Fullback Ned Merriam (who went on to serve as Chicago's varsity track coach for twenty years) repeatedly bungled the play, and after his fourth failure, the exasperated coach declared, "Merriam, you are two jackasses!"[209]

Chicago lost to Carlisle, 18–4. The Indians capped the 1907 campaign by outscoring their opponents 247–62, showcasing their offensive prowess in a 91–0 defeat of a small Lutheran school in rural Pennsylvania named Susquehanna.[210] In that October 2 contest with Susquehanna, Warner's first-year halfback scored four touchdowns, offering the small gathering of spectators a first look at Jim Thorpe—arguably the greatest all-around athlete in history.

Driven to best the records of 1906 and 1907, the Grand Old Man continued to develop new schemes, leaning heavily on the arm of his All-America quarterback Steffen in 1908. Late in the October 31 game against Minnesota, Steffen faked a pass and ran with the ball—the first use of the pass as a "feint"—and the Maroons defeated the Golden Gophers, 29–0.

Two weeks later, Stagg debuted his double-pass play against Cornell. As he described it, "Walter Steffen at quarterback carried the ball as if on an end run. Then he flipped it to Pat Page, who ran back as if to carry it around the other end as he had done previously on his thirty-yard crisscross run. But here we added a cracker to our whip. Left end John Schommer had slipped unnoticed beyond the Cornell secondary and over the goal line while Cornell concentrated on Steffen and Page. Page passed to Schommer for a touchdown."[211] Steffen displayed perfect timing and poise under pressure as he led his team through a driving snow on the game-tying drive in the final minutes.[212]

Steffen and Chicago capped their conference championship 5-0-1 season with an 18–12 defeat of Wisconsin on November 21.[213]

Between 1905 and 1909, Chicago lost only twice—a tribute to the Grand Old Man's ingenuity and to his stars Herschberger, Eckersall and Steffen.[214]

"The championship denied to Stagg that season [1906] was his with interest in 1907 and 1908. Eckersall was gone, but in his stead blossomed another quarterback of All-America stature—Wally Steffen, the original Artful Dodger,"[215] said football historian Allison Danzig.

After Steffen's last game, Stagg declared, "I have never seen Steffen's like as a dodger in cleverness and resourcefulness supported by splendid speed. In running from quarterback, I've never seen anyone who could even approximate his ability. He has more art and finesse in his ball-carrying than Eckersall because Eckie ran chiefly to his right whereas Steffen can run left or right equally well. He is clever at forward passing, deadly in his tackling. He is unusually strong in catching and returning punts. He is a good punter and drop kicker. Above all, he is an inspiring leader and an unsurpassed field general."[216]

Following his graduation, Steffen remained at Chicago, where he served as Stagg's assistant coach while attending law school. After completing his law degree, Steffen was hired as the head football coach at Carnegie Tech (now Carnegie Mellon University) and later became a noted Chicago Superior Court judge.

Alonzo Stagg continued to serve on the Rules Committee until the mid-1950s, during which time he witnessed a sea change in the game he loved and helped to save from almost certain demise. His advocacy on behalf of football established the game's place among the most treasured of American institutions, and his innovations transformed the way football is played.

Stagg did not enjoy unanimous support among his academic colleagues, however. President Harper's January 10, 1906 death signified Stagg's loss of a powerful ally in the administration as tension between opponents of football at the University of Chicago and the head football coach grew. But the university senate's move to abolish football emboldened alumni to increase their support of the Grand Old Man for fear of losing him to another school.[217]

Undeterred by the tumult swirling at Chicago and throughout the game, Stagg continued to lead his boys as he reshaped the game. He held his players to high standards in every phase of their preparation—including their arrival at practice. Any player who failed to arrive fifteen minutes before the scheduled start time was declared late.[218] Stagg expected his players to understand and execute at the highest level and, as such, would not hesitate to repeat a play dozens of times if required. "I do not consider a play learned until the men know it so that everyone knows what to do when it is called. When we can run thru fifty plays with not more than one mistake, then I consider that the men have them mastered."[219]

## Chapter 11

# THE FORWARD PASS ARRIVES
# IN FAYETTEVILLE

**A**s the 1908 Maroons marched toward their second conference title in as many years, Chicago's 1905 championship team standout Hugo Bezdek began his tenure at the University of Arkansas. In the fall of '08, the All-America fullback moved to Fayetteville to take the reins as the school's athletic director and coach of the football, basketball, baseball and track teams.

Bezdek arrived in northwest Arkansas and soon discovered the meager state of the football program he had been hired to lead.[220] Stagg's star pupil sought to manage expectations for the upcoming season as he lamented the condition of his team and the rigorous gridiron schedule that included away games with the University of Oklahoma on October 31 and the University of Texas two days later.[221]

The young coach implemented several changes during his first season, including the establishment of a training table and greater discipline for the squad—imposing the new rules as he surveyed the raw talent of his players with an eye to the future. Arkansas finished 1908 with a respectable 5-4 record that included losses to rivals OU, UT and Louisiana State.[222] The squad's other loss came against Saint Louis University—a 24–0 drubbing resulting from the Billikens' successful use of the forward pass. Coach Eddie Cochems had studied Alonzo Stagg's innovative play and saw its potential to benefit his small but eager athletes. Following the October 17 contest in St. Louis, Bezdek realized the necessity of incorporating the forward pass into his offenses, and he began to retool his playbook. Within a month, the pass had become a small but important addition to Arkansas's running game and overall offensive strategy. In the November 14 contest with Kansas State Normal,[223] Bezdek's squad demonstrated its proficiency defending the forward pass. Behind the arm of quarterback C.L. Sparks and the legs of halfbacks W.J. Nelson, Bert Fleming and C.G. Milford, Arkansas scored seven touchdowns while holding Kansas State Normal to just three field goals.[224] Following the season-ending victory, a local reporter described Bezdek as "quiet and unassuming and possessing the ability to get work out of men where others fail"[225]—clear evidence of the Grand Old Man's influence on the young coach and a foreshadowing of the season ahead.

In his second year, Bezdek's squad avenged the previous season's loss to Oklahoma, dominating the Sooners, 21–6, in their October 30 contest. The matchup pitted Bezdek against Fielding Yost protege Bennie Owen, who quarterbacked Yost's 1899 undefeated Kansas team and in 1901 helped Yost develop the "point-a-minute" system at Michigan before taking the reins at OU in 1905.[226]

Arkansas took a 4-0 record into its eagerly anticipated meeting with Louisiana State in Memphis on November 13. Soon after arriving from Fayetteville on Friday morning, Bezdek had his squad on the field in preparation for the Saturday afternoon game. He ran them through full-speed drills and then finished their workout with swimming at the nearby YMCA pool.[227] Alumni spectators and football critics observed the team's field work and predicted a close contest with an Arkansas victory. Local bookies, however, expected a strong Tiger showing, giving them a two-touchdown advantage.

Warm temperatures and clear skies provided the perfect backdrop as an overflow crowd of two thousand packed Memphis's Red Elm Park. Hundreds of Arkansas fans crossed the Mississippi River to witness the contest, filling the stands with their team's signature red and white. From the opening kickoff, Arkansas's mission to avenge the 1908 loss was clear. "The fighting Cardinals swept the Tigers aside like seaweed before the angry waves of a hurricane on the briny deep," declared a local journalist. Bezdek's run-pass offense kept the LSU defense guessing, behind the leadership of quarterback Steve Creekmore and utility man Stanley Phillip. Two minutes into the game, with Arkansas at the LSU twenty-yard line, Phillip lined up behind Creekmore. Taking the handoff, the fleet-footed back circled the right end and stiff-armed his way through the Louisiana State defense. With six Tiger defenders clinging to his body, Philip ran the steep ascent of the field to the right corner, where he reached the ball just over the goal line.[228] In the second half, Philip added another twenty-yard rushing touchdown following a sixty-yard gain to seal the victory for Bezdek's squad. The crushing defeat of LSU is etched in school history as Arkansas's first ever win over the Tigers— and it's credited by Arkansas faithful for inspiring a legendary nickname. According to University of Arkansas tradition, as his players ran from the field celebrating their victory, Bezdek said they looked like "a wild band of razorback hogs."[229]

Two weeks after Arkansas's defeat of LSU, Stagg traveled to Little Rock to officiate the Thanksgiving Day game between the Razorbacks and Washington University in St. Louis. During his stay, Stagg met with Bezdek to discuss changes to football rules, specifically those related to mass plays. A month earlier, West Point left tackle Eugene Byrne had died as a result of a broken neck he suffered during a mass play run by the Black Knights in their game with Harvard.[230] Both Stagg and Bezdek were troubled by the deaths of Byrne and several college players, and the two agreed that a more open style of play would reduce danger on the field.

The practice of throwing the ball downfield rather than running in a mass formation such as the popular "flying wedge" was still in its infancy, but Bezdek recognized in the pass an opportunity to open the field to create a scoring advantage. He also knew the formations available with passing schemes favored the smaller, faster players whose size left them more vulnerable to injury in grinding run plays. Bezdek and his players had experienced firsthand the dangers of the often brutal run-oriented schemes: Arkansas's fullback and right end, Ernest Dickson, died in November 1908, a week after being kicked in the chest during the Oklahoma game.

As the coaches discussed the forward pass over their Thanksgiving meal, Bezdek recognized a need—and opportunity—to expand his understanding of the offensive tactic.

"Mr. Stagg, my boys and I could use your help," Bezdek declared as he invited his mentor to return to Arkansas to teach his team the technique.

In March 1910, Stagg traveled to the Fayetteville campus to set up his football laboratory. He brought Walter Eckersall along to assist in teaching Bezdek's gridders pass mechanics. For two weeks, the three men experimented with several permutations of the pass play and evaluated the outcomes.

Eckersall and Arkansas quarterback Steve Creekmore "practiced to perfect a pass that would be accurate and effective [as] Stagg and Bezdek directed the workouts of the pair."[231] Bezdek's squad observed the Eckersall and Creekmore demonstrations until Stagg was satisfied; the full squad then ran the drills before the watchful eyes of the Grand Old Man and his protégé, their every movement subject to the evaluation of the play's inventor.

Stagg's stay in Fayetteville yielded solid results for the Razorbacks: the forward pass sped up the game considerably, and beginning that fall, Arkansas used it liberally—and effectively—to dominate stronger run-oriented teams.[232] The two-week clinic also provided useful data for the inventor-coach. Studying the Razorbacks persuaded Stagg to advocate for prohibiting the body-checking of players going after a forward pass.[233] He also determined that passing only to ends rather than to the backfield was the "most acceptable" use of the play, observing that it didn't disadvantage the defense by allowing so many eligible receivers.[234] Stagg reported his findings to the Rules Committee, which used his recommendations to further clarify rules regarding the forward pass as the committee continued to promote advances in the game.

To his own playbook, Stagg modified the man-in-motion he had employed for over a decade by adding a flanker for forward passes. He also created a formation that put the flanker in motion to block the defensive end.[235]

Under Bezdek's leadership during the 1910 season, Creekmore executed the forward pass, often from the spread formation, and through an eight-game campaign, Arkansas outscored its opponents 221–19.[236] "It proved very confusing to our opponents, who had never seen it," Creekmore said of his coach's use of the formation.[237] The Razorbacks also employed Chicago-style shift plays with great success, most notably in their 51–0 season finale crushing of rival LSU.[238]

Bezdek remained at Arkansas for two more seasons. After a brief return to the University of Oregon, he went on to lead the Nittany Lions of Penn State for over a decade and was inducted into the College Football Hall of Fame. The trailblazing coach later served as manager of Major League Baseball's Pittsburgh Pirates and head coach of the National Football League's Cleveland Rams, distinguishing himself as the only man ever to lead a team in both professional sports.

\*\*\*

A year prior to his trip to northwest Arkansas, Alonzo and Stella Stagg became parents for a third time. Their son Paul was born on March 18, 1909, and like his older siblings, the youngest Stagg spent his formative years steeped in football, as his mother diagrammed the plays in their Hyde Park living room that his father's teams executed on the gridiron of Marshall Field.

## Chapter 12

# FROM CHICAGO TO NOTRE DAME

## STAGG, HARPER AND ROCKNE

etween 1905 and 1913, Alonzo Stagg coached three unbeaten teams and five with only one loss.[239] His lone losing season of the period came in 1910, a year in which Illinois held its opponents scoreless and Minnesota gave up only six points in their dominance of the Western Conference.[240]

The tide turned for the Maroons in 1911 as they amassed a 6-1 record, losing only to conference champion Minnesota. Regardless of his teams' results, the Grand Old Man never strayed from his core philosophy of hard work and spartan living. The coach once told a player who had exceeded his meal per diem for an away game, "I'm a stoic, not an epicure," and requested reimbursement for the overage.[241]

Perhaps the only thing in Stagg's life that didn't stay the same was his playbook, as he continued his discipline of examining ways to improve existing plays. In 1913, Stagg filled the early season practices with calisthenics and wind sprints, and in late September he moved to "brain work" in preparation for the Western Conference gauntlet. The head Maroon provided his charges with a half dozen new plays and observed their mastery in a series of inter-squad scrimmages leading up to the season opener.

"I'm ready to concentrate on the plays intended for the game against Indiana. The boys are in better physical condition than I have seen a squad at this stage in three years," Stagg said to the fans gathered outside the gates of the practice field.[242] The preseason drills featured especially strong performances by center Paul Des Jardien and end Stan

Baumgartner—two players blessed with physical stature to complement their athletic abilities.

In 1912, a six-foot, one-inch Stan "Lefty" Baumgartner made the leap from scrub to starter, earning his place on the varsity despite knowing nothing of football prior to enrolling at Chicago. A standout in basketball, baseball and track, Baumgartner so impressed Stagg that the head Maroon took a special interest in teaching him the gridiron game. "It is his eagerness to do things that makes me think so much of him. He is a hog for work, and when he is put to doing anything you can depend upon him," the coach said.[243]

At six feet, five inches and 190 pounds, Des Jardien looked every bit like a basketball center, another position he played for Stagg. But "Shorty" Des Jardien possessed abilities that helped him adapt to any sport, as evidenced by his work at center for the football team, which earned him first team All-Western honors in 1912.

"Stagg's Afraid of Purdue" was a frequent headline in Chicago-area papers each fall in the lead-up to the Maroons' game against the Boilermakers. In 1913, Stagg's boys took it to heart. The Maroon head man had traveled to West Lafayette to study Purdue in its game against Northwestern on October 11. What he and the other scouts on hand witnessed was a near-perfect exhibition of football prowess as the Purple[244] fell, 34–0.[245] Purdue halfback Elmer "Ollie" Oliphant scored a touchdown and three field goals in the effort, as the Indianapolis press declared him "faster and harder to handle than ever before," and Purdue faithful pinned on him their hopes for victories against conference foes Wisconsin and Chicago.[246]

The Boilermakers had not beaten the Maroons in over a decade, but each year, Chicago's margin of victory decreased; as the 1913 showdown with Chicago approached, many in West Lafayette believed new head coach Andy Smith and his squad would turn the tables.[247] After the visitors arrived at Marshall Field for their final pregame practice, Smith expressed confidence in his squad's readiness: "We will win, unless the men are attacked by stage fright or tremble at the sight of the tall buildings, and I do not think that will happen."[248]

The October 25 contest in Chicago was the day's marquee match-up of Western Conference schools, positioning the victor as the favorite to claim the league's championship.[249] Fans arrived early at the 57th Street and Ellis Avenue ticket windows to purchase the remaining seats, leaving hundreds of latecomers, including future White Sox owner Louis Comiskey, astonished to discover the game was a sellout.[250]

Stagg's reconnaissance had persuaded him to create a defensive strategy for Purdue's star halfback that ran through the Maroon big man, Des Jardien. Stagg instructed Des Jardien to play "free" center on defense—standing up straight and looking for the fleet-footed Boilermaker. From the opening series, the five-foot, seven-inch, 158-pound Oliphant could find no daylight before Des Jardien brought him down. Des Jardien and the Maroon defense contained Purdue's star, limiting him to minimal gains in the first half, but a Chicago fumble, two offensive interference penalties and an interception kept the home team from the end zone. The teams traded punts, and as the clock wound down on the first quarter, the Maroons began a drive from midfield. Baumgartner gained twenty-five yards on a forward pass. Successive end-around runs by quarterback Russell and halfback Norgren gained another fifteen yards. Three rushing attempts failed to advance the ball, and Russell kicked a go-ahead field goal. Late in the first quarter, Oliphant stood ready to punt on fourth down. He fielded the snap, tucked the ball and ran for a twelve-yard gain before being upended by a Maroon defender. After landing on his head, the dazed Oliphant regained his footing and began to run toward his own goal line. Chicago defenders looked on in amused surprise as the wayward rusher gained four yards before being stopped by a teammate. The safety-saving tackle brought an end to the peculiar play and to the first quarter.[251]

Oliphant regained his bearings during the brief intermission, and Coach Smith called his number on three consecutive running plays to start the second quarter. Chicago held him to six total yards, and on fourth down, Oliphant again attempted a fake punt. Chicago anticipated the run and stopped him for no gain at the forty-yard line. Each team allowed minimal gains before forcing the other to punt the ball. With four minutes left in the half, Chicago's Paul Russell fielded a Purdue kick at the Maroon forty-five-yard line. With a burst of speed, he maneuvered around his blockers before being brought down at the Boilermaker twenty-two. In the second play of the series, left end John Vruwink ran a short crossing route, and Russell dropped back to pass. As the ball sailed over the line, Purdue's right end stepped in front of Vruwink and intercepted the pass at the twenty-yard line. Oliphant made a series of short gains that created momentum for the visitors, but as he emerged from the pile near midfield, a whistle signaled the end of the half.[252]

In a defensive performance that surprised even Stagg himself, Des Jardien allowed Oliphant no rushing yardage in the second half. Purdue changed its strategy late in the fourth quarter and attempted a series of forward passes, advancing to the Maroon thirty-yard line when Oliphant launched the ball toward the goal line. Chicago's Nelson Norgren read the play and intercepted the pass as time expired.[253]

The 1913 Maroons finished 7-0, won the conference championship and surrendered a total of only twenty-seven points.[254] Des Jardien was named to the All-America and All-Western teams, and Walter Camp called him "the best center in the country."[255] Along with his teammate Baumgartner, Des Jardien earned letters in four sports during each of his three years as a varsity athlete, placing the two in the rarified air of multi-year, multi-sport "C" men.[256]

Beginning in 1913, when Stagg called a player's number during a game, he did so quite literally. The Grand Old Man began the practice of numbering players' jerseys, a move that spectators, particularly those in the press, cheered. The use of visible identifiers gained popularity throughout college football, and nearly a quarter century later, in 1937, the College Football Rules Committee codified the practice by requiring players to wear numbers on the front and back of their jerseys.[257]

After leaving Chicago, Des Jardien played professional football for the Cleveland Indians of the Ohio League, the Chicago Tigers of the American Professional Football Association and the Minneapolis Marines of the National Football League.[258] He also played one season of professional baseball for the Cleveland Indians, putting him in an elite fraternity of men who played both professional baseball and professional football.[259]

During the year following his graduation, Des Jardien traveled with the Maroon baseball team to Japan for an international series in Tokyo, a practice Stagg had begun three years earlier. Former Maroon team captain Fred Merrifield helped introduce baseball to the Japanese in the early 1900s when he served as coach of the University of Waseda ball club, and he invited his former coach to schedule games with universities on the island nation.[260] Upon the team's return home, Des Jardien remained on the Midway to serve as an assistant coach of the baseball, track and basketball teams.[261]

Many of Stagg's former players followed in his footsteps, leading athletic teams at the collegiate level. In 1915, the list numbered at least twenty:[262]

Phillip Arbuckle: Rice Institute (Houston, Texas)
Hugo Bezdek: University of Oregon (Eugene, Oregon)
Mark Catlin: Lawrence College (Appleton, Wisconsin)
Paul Des Jardien: University of Chicago (Chicago, Illinois)

Leo DeTray: Knox College (Galesburg, Illinois)
Ivan Doseff: Fargo College (Fargo, North Dakota)
Sherman Finger: Cornell College (Mount Vernon, Iowa)
Jesse Harper: University of Notre Dame (South Bend, Indiana)
Earl Huntington: University of Chicago (Chicago, Illinois)
Thomas Kelley: University of Alabama (Tuscaloosa, Alabama)
Walter Kennedy: Albion College (Albion, Michigan)
John Koehler: Marquette University (Milwaukee, Wisconsin)
Nelson Norgren: University of Utah (Salt Lake City, Utah)
Pat Page: University of Chicago (Chicago, Illinois)
Norman Paine: University of Chicago (Chicago, Illinois)
Charles Rademacher: University of Idaho (Moscow, Idaho)
Clarence Russell: New Mexico College of Agriculture and Mechanical Arts
    (Las Cruces, New Mexico)
Walter Steffen: Carnegie Institute (Pittsburgh, Pennsylvania)
Herman Stegeman: Beloit College (Beloit, Wisconsin)
Horace Whiteside: Earlham College (Richmond, Indiana)

As Alonzo Stagg ran his squad through gymnastics in the summer of 1913, one of his former players-turned-coach labored over a football schedule intended to fill the bleachers—and the coffers—of his new gridiron home. In 1913, Jesse Harper left Wabash College for another small, private, all-male institution in rural Indiana.[263] Administrators, as well as students and alumni, at the University of Notre Dame were eager to increase the strength and revenues of the athletic program, and as such, they looked to another Stagg disciple to lead the program in a positive direction. Like Irish legend Frank Hering before him, Harper learned his craft on Chicago's Midway under the tutelage of Alonzo Stagg. Harper started in the Chicago backfield with Hugo Bezdek and served ably as a backup for the All-America quarterback Walter Eckersall. Though often overshadowed by the legendary Eckersall, Harper made his mark during the Maroons' undefeated national championship campaign of 1905, scoring three rushing touchdowns in the defeat of Iowa.[264]

Harper worked to secure games with competitive opponents, but conflicts within the Western Conference forced the new coach to look beyond the Midwest to fill his team's dance card—a fortuitous complication for Notre Dame, as it turned out. The 1913 schedule was the most difficult in the school's history, and it required Harper's men to face six teams they had never seen before.[265]

Notre Dame opened the season with three home games, two of which the squad won handily. The third, an October 18 date with South Dakota, required some late-game heroics to secure a 20–7 victory.[266]

On November 1, Notre Dame traveled to West Point, New York, to face Army. Quarterback Gus Dorais and end Knute Rockne famously employed the forward pass to secure a 35–13 victory over the Cadets. Harper's two veterans elevated Stagg's innovative play to renown en route to an undefeated season and All-Western team honors.

Over the next four years in South Bend, Harper compiled a 34-5-1 record. Harper's most significant and lasting gift to Notre Dame athletics, however, was his advocacy on behalf of the man who would replace him as head football coach. Following the 1917 season, Harper informed the university's president, Father John W. Cavanaugh, of his decision to resign in order to assume management of his family's Kansas ranch from his ailing father-in-law. In a negotiation not unlike the one between William Rainey Harper and Alonzo Stagg at the Murray Hill Hotel twenty-seven years earlier, Jesse Harper (no relation to the University of Chicago president) championed his pick for a successor. After nearly two weeks of debate between Notre Dame's president and its head football coach, Harper played what proved to be his trump card. Father Cavanaugh acquiesced, despite his concerns over the prospective coach's youth and temperament, when Harper informed him that several years earlier Harper had promised his man the position.

"Well, Jesse, if you promised it to him, we certainly will have to offer it to him, won't we?" Cavanaugh blithely responded. The following week, Knute Rockne signed a contract to become Notre Dame's head football and athletic director.[267]

Years later, when asked about the origins of the "Notre Dame system," Rockne didn't hesitate in his reply: "The game which I have taught, with some important changes, was brought to Notre Dame by Jesse Harper, whom I succeeded in 1918. Harper was one of Alonzo Stagg's best quarterbacks at Chicago. Stagg brought his game from Yale. Ergo, just as we all trace back to Adam, so does Notre Dame football go back to Stagg and to Yale."[268]

*Chapter 13*

# RAISING BOYS

**A**pplause filled the ballroom, and Fritz Crisler knew immediately that Mr. Stagg had arrived. Standing across the room, Crisler turned his back to the entrance and quickly removed the lit cigarette from his lips, wrapped it in his palm and put his hands in his pockets.[269]

It was 1959, and the Chicago men were gathered for a celebration of the "C" Club. Stagg had traveled from Stockton, California, where at age ninety-six, he was in the waning days of his coaching career, working as an assistant coach at Stockton College. Fritz Crisler arrived from Ann Arbor, where he served as the University of Michigan's athletic director. As the cigarette smoldered in his pocket, Crisler recalled a conversation with his coach earlier that year at the meeting of the NCAA Football Rules Committee. At the conclusion of the meeting, the fifty-nine-year-old Crisler stood before the assembled members to thank his friend and mentor for his wise counsel on behalf of the committee. "We've had a wonderful time," Stagg responded as he prepared to leave. Crisler's former coach then shook his hand and said, "Behave yourself."[270] Stagg's admonition to his boys to at all times "behave yourself" certainly included no smoking.[271]

Forty-two years earlier, a skinny freshman who could have been blown over by the winds off Lake Michigan walked absentmindedly across the University of Chicago campus. "Run the end sweep again, and this time show me some blocking, Higgins," barked Stagg. Gale Blocki took the snap from James Reber and made a clean handoff to Bernard MacDonald on the end around. The swift right end swept wide around the line behind a block from Charles Higgins. Stagg darted to his left to avoid a collision with MacDonald, and he ran directly into the unsuspecting student who had wandered onto the practice field.

"If you're going to play football," quipped Stagg as he helped a dazed Herbert Crisler to his feet, "why don't you put on a suit?" The freshman from Earlsville, Illinois, who enrolled at the University of Chicago with an academic scholarship and plans for a career in medicine took the head coach up on his offer.

After a few days on the practice field, however, Crisler decided to abandon football in favor of his pre-med studies. Walking across campus the following week, Stagg encountered Crisler. "I would never have picked you for a quitter." Crisler bristled at the remark and returned to the football field. "I've been in athletics ever since," Crisler quipped in an interview some fifty years later.

Stagg again demonstrated a keen ability to identify raw talent and motivate a player, as he followed the inauspicious start to Crisler's football career with the assignment of an ignominious nickname. During practice, after Crisler's mistakes at the left end position caused four consecutive plays to fail, the head coach called him aside. "Crisler, from now on you are 'Fritz,' after the master violinist. Not because you resemble him, but because you are so different."[272]

Stagg had thrown down the gauntlet, and Crisler responded. The young scholar became a standout on the freshman team in 1917, leading his eleven to a 13–7 victory in the inter-squad "Yale-Harvard" game during Thanksgiving week. Crisler gained a few pounds, grew a few inches and earned a starting spot on the varsity team as a sophomore.

Crisler went on to earn nine varsity letters at Chicago in football, basketball and baseball. In 1921, he was named to the College Football All-America team by Walter Camp.[273] And were it not for his frequent chapel absences, Crisler would have been elected to Phi Beta Kappa his senior year.[274]

Following his graduation, Crisler remained at Chicago for nearly a decade as Stagg's gridiron assistant. In 1930, he left the Midway for Minnesota, where he served as the Golden Gophers' head football coach and athletic director. After two seasons in Minneapolis, Crisler took the reins of football and baseball at Princeton. But it was in 1938, when he moved to Ann Arbor, that Crisler embarked on an extraordinary thirty-year career building Michigan into the athletic powerhouse it remains more than eighty years later. Don Canham, when he was hired to replace the retiring Crisler as Michigan's athletic director in 1968, expressed equal parts joy and apprehension. "I'm quite happy, naturally [but] I have a few qualms about succeeding Mr. Crisler. It's a little like stepping up to bat after Babe Ruth."[275]

\*\*\*

The Stagg children early on embraced the game their parents loved. As soon as Paul was old enough to grip a football and attempt a forward pass, he and Alonzo Jr. ("Lonnie") were playing catch. What began in the living room of the Stagg home eventually—and out of necessity—moved outside.

Football transcended the brothers' ten-year age difference, and playing it forged a bond between the two. That bond extended to the gridiron of the Midway, where they studied their father's teams, practicing the plays their mother artfully diagrammed. As young men, both of the Stagg brothers played for the coaching legend on the field that bore his name. Decades later and hundreds of miles from their Chicago home, they would face off as college coaches.

Before he even graduated from high school, Lonnie had earned a graduate degree in the psychology of coaching. He studied in the laboratory of Stagg Field with the dean of college football coaches and witnessed the well-chosen words of a coach inspiring good players to become great ones.

The namesake of the venerable coach dedicated equal time to studying the charts and diagrams of the Maroons' plays. Every Sunday after church, the Stagg children spread a copy of the *Chicago Tribune* on the Staggs' living room floor. Throughout Alonzo Stagg's tenure as head coach at Chicago, the *Tribune*'s sports editor published Stella's diagrams of the Maroons' plays from the previous day's game in the Sunday edition. Lonnie, Ruth and Paul carefully studied the images, often asking Stella questions as she washed the Sunday dinner dishes. When they felt sufficiently confident in their mastery of the plays, the young Staggs trotted out to the front yard to practice them.

Stella saved the play diagrams—along with every article written about Alonzo and his Maroons. Lonnie carefully organized the diagrams in a scrapbook that became the football Bible whose verses he and Paul memorized. Stella's painstaking preservation of articles, correspondence and memorabilia from Alonzo Stagg's life and career provided the University of Chicago with over three hundred boxes of materials, which it has catalogued and preserved as the Amos Alonzo Stagg Papers, housed in its archives.[276]

Like the rest of her family, Lonnie and Paul's sister, Ruth, loved football. She was not afraid to join in a pick-up game with her father and brothers. And the elder Stagg was as eager to teach her the game as he was for his sons to learn to play it.

"Ruthie, I am a teacher," he often told his daughter. "The most important job I have is to teach you, your brothers and all of the boys who play for me. God gave me football as the way to teach hard work and self-discipline. Those are important lessons for you, so I want you to understand the game."

Lonnie and Paul Stagg spent every available minute playing sports; most often, it was a game of football with friends in the family's front yard. What Lonnie discovered in his early school age, Paul came to appreciate as well: the turf grass of the Staggs' lawn provided a perfect field for neighborhood football games. Coach Stagg gladly performed the duties of groundskeeper each evening following the boys' neighborhood games.

"You can't grow grass, Mr. Stagg, unless you keep those kids off it," offered a neighbor as he watched the Maroon coach once again repair his worn lawn. As Stagg replaced the torn divots dotting the yard, he thanked him for his concern and replied, "We're not trying to raise grass. We're trying to raise boys."[277]

## Chapter 14

# THE JACKASS CLUB

When a young man received an offer to play for Alonzo Stagg, he did so with a clear understanding of the coach's expectations for on- and off-the-field conduct. Stagg tolerated no smoking, no drinking and no cussing. The Grand Old Man held his players to the same standards he held himself, knowing that when accompanied by his training regimen, those ideals would produce men of character.

Stagg's prohibition against foul language did not prevent him from employing a caustic vocabulary, however. In the event a player committed a boneheaded mistake, he was certain to earn a vociferous response from the head coach. Most likely, Stagg would call the offending player a "jackass" and describe, without any ambiguity, what he expected the player to do to correct the mistake.

So reliable was Stagg in applying the epithet that his players established the Jackass Club, and they designated as its president the first man of the season to be tagged with the pejorative.[278] To be termed a jackass conveyed only common membership to the player. If Stagg found an on-the-field offense particularly egregious, he clarified his degree of displeasure with the distinction *long-eared jackass* or *double jackass*.

The charter member of Stagg's Chicago stable of jackasses was John Schommer.[279] That the stellar four-sport athlete was included in the infamous cadre proved no one was immune to the coach's particular invective.

By his fourth year at Chicago, Schommer had earned the nickname "Mr. Everything" for his achievements in football, basketball, baseball and track.[280] The Maroons' first twelve-letter recipient set an indoor high jump world record, earned conference top scorer honors three seasons on the hardwood, proved his mettle on the diamond by winning a conference batting title with a .475 average and was named an all-conference end as a two-time Big Ten gridiron champion.[281] Chants of "Scho Knows!" no doubt would have echoed from the Midway had Schommer been born eighty years later and offered athletic apparel endorsements.

But in 1908, the Maroons opened their season against the Boilermakers with a familiar chorus of headlines reading "Stagg Fears Purdue."[282] The Grand Old Man worked his playbook from cover to cover in an effort to keep the Boilermaker defense guessing. Early in the first half, Schommer lined up at left end and Pat Page at right end. Quarterback Wally Steffen barked the call and received the snap from center. Schommer ran back to the right, taking the handoff from Steffen as Page crossed behind the defense and sprinted down the middle of the field. Schommer eyed the streaking Page and sent the ball sailing into the air. It landed squarely on the twenty-yard line, ten yards beyond the waiting receiver with a clear path to the end zone.

"John, you are now two jackasses!"[283] Stagg exclaimed as Schommer reached the sideline following the play. Perhaps spurred by the ignominious distinction of being labeled a double jackass, Schommer scored two rushing touchdowns and kicked 5 extra points and one field goal in the second half as Chicago defeated Purdue 39–0.[284]

A decade later, Fritz Crisler achieved a previously unreached zenith of Stagg's invective. According to his teammate Schommer, "Fritz was elevated above the rank and file of jackasses when he repeatedly bungled the play on succeeding downs. As Fritz's mistakes accumulated, Stagg promoted him from jackass to double jackass and finally King of Jackasses."[285]

Stagg did not limit the club's membership to Chicago students, as evidenced when two members of the famed Four Horsemen of Notre Dame found themselves tagged with his epithet.[286]

In their October 1923 bout with Army, the Irish emerged victorious, but stars Harry Stuhldreher and Elmer Leyden were injured in the process. Having heard about a trainer at the University of Chicago widely regarded for his ability to repair strained ligaments, Notre Dame's Knute Rockne asked Stagg's permission to send the boys to the Midway for treatment. Stagg gladly consented, and the two arrived at the Chicago campus on Monday morning.

Local high school football players would also schedule treatment with the trainer on Mondays. On this particular day, however, Stuhldreher and Leyden were the only ones seeking aid. As they waited, Stagg walked into the gym.

"Hello, boys. What high school are you from?" the Old Man asked.

Stuhldreher glanced casually at his teammate and replied, "Hyde Park."

"You boys did great work last Saturday beating Wendell Phillips." Stagg added, "We would like to see some of you come to Chicago."

"Thank you, Sir," replied Leyden, suppressing a smile.

About that time, Rockne walked into the gym. "Knute, where are those two boys who walloped Army?" Stagg asked as the two men shook hands.

"Here they are," replied Rockne, pointing to the pair sitting on the bench.

Stagg furrowed his brow, glared at Stuhldreher and Leyden and hissed, "Jackasses."

## Chapter 15

# FOOTBALL ON THE AIRWAVES

**D**espite the presence of Crisler on the varsity roster, the Maroons struggled much of the 1920 season, finishing the year with four straight conference losses, including shutouts against Illinois, Michigan and Wisconsin.[287] Fortunately for Stagg and company, a star was waiting in the wings.

Prior to the start of the 1920 season, All–Rocky Mountain halfback Milton "Mitt" Romney had transferred from the University of Utah to Chicago to play for the Grand Old Man.[288] Long before his cousin and namesake would rescue the 2002 Salt Lake Winter Olympics from financial calamity and go on to be elected governor of Massachusetts, the elder Romney achieved his own fame in the backfield of the Utah gridiron. Eligibility rules required Romney to play on the freshman team his first year at Chicago before joining the Maroon varsity. During his year on the green team, the Utah native scored 34 points in two contests with the Maroon varsity, demonstrating his strength as a kicker and a rusher.[289]

After the 1920 campaign, Stagg's twenty-one-member varsity squad lost 10 "C" men, and the Grand Old Man eagerly welcomed Romney to the team.[290] Armed with his tin whistle and pointed vocabulary, Stagg entered his thirtieth season at the Maroons' helm with well-placed, furtive optimism.[291] In the 1921 season opener, Romney lived up to advance billing, proving a triple threat with his skills in punting, passing and running, as he led Chicago to a 41–0 rout of Northwestern.[292] Three weeks later, the underdog Maroons traveled to New Jersey for a meeting with a vaunted Princeton team that viewed the game as little more than a warm-up for its contests with eastern foes Harvard and Yale. The famed writer Damon Runyon looked on as "the Utah Flash" had his way with the Tiger defense, declaring that Romney "chilled the football hopes of Princeton this afternoon like an icy blast off Lake Michigan, but he left behind him the memory of his war cry, 'Go, Chicago.'"[293] Romney accounted for the game's only scores—running for a touchdown and booting a field goal—to seal a 9–0 win in the battle of West versus East.[294] In the season's final contest, Romney drop-kicked a field goal from the seventeen-yard line to preserve a 3–0 win over Wisconsin.[295] Chicago's only loss came on November 5 to Ohio State: with a fourth-quarter touchdown, the Buckeyes won the defensive battle, 7–0. Chicago finished the season with a 7-1 record that included 5 shutout wins, behind Romney's passing, running and kicking and Crisler's receiving.[296] The Maroons surrendered only 13 points during the 1921 season, tied with Wisconsin for the lowest total points allowed among the nation's 102 collegiate football programs.[297] Walter Eckersall selected both Chicago stars to his All–Western Conference squads—Crisler on the first team and Romney on the second.[298]

The United Press named the "Mormon State Zephyr" second-team All–Western Conference quarterback.[299] Romney's teammates elected him captain for the following season.[300] Academic ineligibility rendered him unable to take the field in the fall of 1922, however. So eager for learning was Romney that he earned enough credits to graduate in June, a year ahead of schedule.[301] The unexpected dilemma forced Stagg to establish a competition for the job among the underclassmen, one of whom was his son, Alonzo "Lonnie" Stagg Jr.

Romney graduated and left Chicago for Austin, where the University of Texas hired him as its head basketball and baseball coach and assistant football and track coach.[302] The following year, he returned to the Midwest to play professional football for the fledgling NFL—first for the Racine Legion and then for George Halas's Chicago Bears, where he played quarterback for four seasons.[303]

In 1922, Lonnie Stagg Jr. shared quarterback duties with Otto Strohmeier, John Burgess and Lewis McMasters. The Maroon squad finished 5-1-1 in a season highlighted by shutouts of Georgia, Purdue and Illinois.[304]

On October 28, the Princeton Tigers traveled to the Midway with hopes of avenging the previous season's humiliating home loss to the Maroons. The clash of East–West giants did not disappoint—and it was made available for a coast-to-coast audience in the first-ever radio broadcast of a college football game.[305]

Princeton entered the game 4-0, having surrendered no points to its opponents.[306] Experts picked the Tigers to lose each week, but Princeton found ways to win despite the fact that, as halfback Charlie Caldwell described his team, "We had no blocking. We couldn't make a first down at times if we tried to. We had no forward passing to speak of." What the team had in spades, however, were brains and grit. "[Coach Bill] Roper felt that football was 90 percent fight," said Caldwell, "and all the rest was 10 percent."[307]

Chicago pounded the Tiger defensive line and, without employing a single forward pass, scored a touchdown in each of the first three quarters. Early in the final period, Princeton punt returner John Gorman attempted a lateral toss to teammate Jack Cleaves that was ruled an illegal forward pass. After the penalty was assessed, the Tigers stood ninety-eight yards from the goal line. Chicago's defense stiffened and forced Princeton into the familiar position of punting from near its own end zone. With twelve minutes remaining in the game, Chicago held an 18–7 lead and appeared poised for victory.[308]

Momentum turned for the Tigers, however, when an errant snap from the Maroons' back-up center to quarterback Willis Zorn ricocheted off the quarterback's shoulder and into the hands of Princeton left end Howdy Gray, who sprinted forty-two yards downfield for a touchdown.[309] Minutes later, Princeton successfully executed a fake punt and marched down the field to score a go-ahead touchdown. The committee of quarterbacks and their Chicago teammates responded with a combination of forward passes and long rushes that pushed the Tiger defense back on its heels. With seconds remaining in the game, Chicago assembled at the threshold of the end zone with the ball on the one-yard line. Stagg Jr. stood on the sideline with his father and watched—along with thirty-two thousand spectators—as Maroon back John Thomas took the handoff, hugged the ball and charged forward, leaping over the right tackle of the Princeton line. As he fell forward, Thomas was met by a wave of the Tiger defensive secondary. The bodies slowly emerged from the pile until Thomas was visible on the field—one foot short of the goal line. With a final score of 21–18, Princeton handed Chicago its only loss of the 1922 campaign.[310] "The wonders of wireless technology were never better exemplified," remarked a Princeton alumnus who listened to the radio broadcast of the game.[311] The victory served as a springboard for the rest of the season as the Tigers—termed the "Team of Destiny" by Grantland Rice—went undefeated and claimed a national championship.[312]

***

The following spring, Lonnie Stagg Jr. received his degree from the University of Chicago. While visiting Harvard as he prepared to enter graduate school, Stagg walked through the picturesque Cambridge campus and was met by a university dean. As the two talked, Harvard's dean expressed amazement that Stagg would choose Harvard over his father's alma mater, Yale. For the next two hours, the dean proceeded to tell Young Stagg of his father's exploits on the baseball diamond. "Harvard was never so glad to see a young man graduate from Yale."[313]

*Chapter 16*

# THE STAGG ERA AT CHICAGO
# DRAWS TO A CLOSE

C hicago's November 8, 1924 date with Robert Zuppke's Fighting Illini presented a monumental task for Stagg and his squad. Illinois entered the game undefeated, and three weeks earlier, Illini legend Harold "Red" Grange had single-handedly torn through the vaunted University of Michigan defense. In the first twelve minutes of the Wolverine contest, Grange scored four touchdowns: a ninety-five-yard opening kickoff return and runs of sixty-seven, fifty-six and forty-four yards. "The Galloping Ghost" added an eleven-yard touchdown run in the second half and, for good measure, threw a twenty-yard touchdown pass to lead his team to a 39–14 victory over a Michigan team unbeaten in its previous twenty games.[314] The epic performance—the most remarkable in football history and at the Wolverines' expense—was enough to bring coach Fielding Yost out of his one-year retirement from coaching.[315]

Stagg reasoned that the Maroons could combat Zuppke's "Grange Formation" by denying the Illini offense and its star the opportunity to handle the ball. Chicago's offense executed the plan perfectly in the first quarter as Maroon fullback Austin McCarty repeatedly pounded through an Illinois defense that gave up fifteen pounds per man to the Chicago line. The Maroon fullback's succession of short gains led to three touchdowns in the first half and earned him the nickname "Five-Yard" McCarty. Early in the second quarter, Grange seized an opening and marched the Illini down the field for a touchdown on a series of forward passes and long runs. Then in the final minutes of the half, Illinois's Earl Britton, from a field goal formation, tossed the ball to Chuck Kassell, who lateraled to Grange, who then sprinted down the sideline to the four-yard line. On the next play, Grange took the handoff and raced around the left end for a touchdown, cutting the Maroon lead to 21–14 at the half.[316]

The third quarter opened to strong defensive stands by both teams, with Illinois's backfield box defense particularly effective in stopping Chicago's forward progress. Midway through the period, a quick kick by Chicago's Graham Kernwein forced Illinois to start from its own twenty-yard line. On the first play from scrimmage, Grange shot around the left end, down the sideline and then back to the middle through downfield blocks for an eighty-yard score. Both offenses were again stymied in the fourth quarter, as each team failed to convert field goal attempts. In the closing seconds of the game, Chicago's Robert Curley fielded an Illini punt but was downed at midfield as the final whistle blew.

Given the pregame expectations, the final score of 21–21 was a stunning achievement for Stagg and the Maroons. Grange, Stagg and Walter Camp all later reflected on the game:

*The Illinois-Chicago classic of 1924 was the toughest football game I ever played in college. Every time I was tackled, I was hit hard by two or three men. At one point in the game I was so exhausted I fell flat on my face as the Maroons were running off a play. I was no exception, for the entire Illinois team took a terrific beating. I don't believe the Illini in my day had ever been in such a ferocious football game.—Grange*

*Taken all in all—the expected one-sided victory, the over-shadowing reputation of Grange, the irresistible sweep of Chicago from the kick-off, the tremendous upset in the first quarter, the seesaw in the second quarter, Grange's magnificent response in which he brought the Illinois score from 0 to 21 virtually single-handed, the breathless dead-lock in the final quarter, with both teams narrowly denied the winning touchdown, made it one of the greatest football dramas ever played on any field.—Stagg*

*Harold Grange is the marvel of this year's [1924 All-America] backfield. His work in the Michigan game was a revelation, but his performance in the Chicago game went even further when by his play-running and forward passing he accounted for some 450 yards of territory. He is elusive, has a baffling change of pace, a good straight arm and finally seems in some way to get a map of the field at starting and then threads his way through his opponents.—Camp*[317]

The Maroons finished the season 3-0-3 in conference play and 4-1-3 overall. Their 1924 Western Conference championship would be the last of the Stagg era. Between 1925 and 1932, Maroon gridiron teams struggled to compete against major schools as the university deemphasized intercollegiate athletics in favor of attracting the academic elite to the Midway. During the eight-year period, Chicago posted a winning record in only one season.[318] Paul Stagg, the youngest of Stella and Alonzo's three children, joined his father on the Midway gridiron from 1929 to 1931, when he played quarterback, halfback and receiver.

A bright spot in an otherwise dim period on the Midway was the addition of Jay Berwanger to the Maroon squad. He enrolled at the University of Chicago in 1932 and played just one season for Stagg, but he reflected the coach's keen ability to identify talent and refine it with hard work.[319]

Stagg won the recruiting battle against Michigan, Minnesota, Purdue and Iowa for the all-state halfback from Dubuque. In 1932, with the United States in the throes of the Great Depression, Chicago offered Berwanger a basic tuition scholarship of $300 per year, which he eagerly accepted to, in his words, "attend a school that would give me a first-rate education in business…so that I would be prepared when opportunities were certain to return." To pay his expenses, the young Berwanger waited tables, cleaned the school's gym and fixed leaking toilets when he wasn't in the classroom or on the practice field.[320]

During the first five conference games of his sophomore year, Berwanger played every down, as a halfback, receiver, defensive back or kicker.[321] In a season where the Maroons finished 3-3-2, Berwanger did it all, because his team needed him to. The following year, the Maroon great led his team to a 4-0 start before an injury against Purdue left him with a bruised knee that turned the tide on Chicago's season. Despite his impairment, Berwanger returned to the field against Minnesota and Michigan. In the last game of the 1934 season, the Chicago halfback delivered a memorable blow to the face of a Wolverine defender. "When I tackled Jay one time, his heel hit my cheekbone and opened it up three inches,"[322] said the Michigan great who would become the leader of the free world four decades later. In a conversation many years after the game, President Gerald Ford joked with Berwanger about the scar under his left eye. "I think of you every morning when I shave."[323]

In November 1935, Chicago's outstanding halfback, quarterback, kicker and defender received a telegram from the Downtown Athletic Club of New York informing him he had been selected the "most valuable football player east of the Mississippi."[324] Jay Berwanger received eighty-four total points in the voting, winning in a runaway against Army's Monk Meyer (twenty-nine points), Notre Dame's William Shakespeare (twenty-three points) and Princeton's Pepper Constable (twenty points). Willard Prince, the first publisher and editor of the *D.A.C. Journal*, devised the voting formula, still in use by the Heisman Trust, designed to prevent regional biases from determining the winner.

Earlier that year, Prince met with several renowned sculptors of the day to discuss the trophy and its design. Each one turned down the job. His options limited, Prince found a twenty-three-year-old recent graduate of Brooklyn's Pratt Institute. Many years later, the sculptor would earn fame as creator of the *Cascade of Books* adorning the entrance of the James Madison Memorial Building of the Library of Congress. But it was his first commission—for which he was paid $200—that established Frank Eliscu's legacy.

Prince gave Eliscu only one piece of guidance: create a trophy of a football player in action. The artist fashioned three wax mock-ups, and Prince asked the DAC's president, John Heisman, Columbia University's Lou Little and Fordham University's Jim Crowley (of Notre Dame's fabled Four Horsemen) to select one of Eliscu's designs. They unanimously selected Eliscu's least favorite: the now iconic straight-armed runner. The artist preferred his rendition of a lineman tackling a ball carrier but acquiesced to the wishes of the football experts. Each of the men requested tweaks to the design, requiring Eliscu to search for inspiration in crafting the statue's details. Eliscu turned to the pages of the newspaper, where, prophetically, he found a picture of Jay Berwanger in action.[325]

In 1936, the Downtown Athletic Club Trophy was renamed to honor the DAC's president, John Heisman. The famed coach of Auburn, Clemson and, most notably, Georgia Tech insisted that the award not bear his name, but following his October 3 death, Edith Maora Heisman agreed to the DAC's request to rename the trophy for her late husband.[326] Beginning with Jay Berwanger and continuing through the present day, the men who have earned membership in this exclusive fraternity are, regardless of any of their other accomplishments, always described with the modifier "Heisman Trophy winner."

As he prepared to graduate from Chicago in 1936, Jay Berwanger made football history again: he was named the first selection in the first National Football League draft. The Philadelphia Eagles, by virtue of their last-place finish the previous season, held the first draft pick. Unsure they could meet the Maroon utility man's salary expectations of $1,000 per game, the Eagles traded Berwanger to the Chicago Bears.[327] Berwanger asked George Halas for $15,000 per year, which the legendary Bears coach countered with an offer of $13,500. The impasse marked the only time in twenty years that Coach Halas failed to secure a college player he sought.[328] Halas and Berwanger parted ways over $1,500, and the "One-Man Team," as he was affectionately known at the University of Chicago, never played a down of professional football; instead, he accepted a position as a foam rubber salesman and served as a part-time assistant football coach at his alma mater under head coach Clark Shaughnessy.

Berwanger and Shaughnessy remained at Chicago until 1939, when the university's president, Dr. Robert Maynard Hutchins, disbanded the football program.

Seven years earlier, on December 5, 1932, a seventy-year-old Alonzo Stagg was relieved of his head coaching duties at the University of Chicago. The decision was made, ostensibly, by the school's new athletic director, T. Nelson Metcalf; but in point of fact, President Hutchins compelled Metcalf to enforce the university's age-mandated retirement policy with Stagg. Hutchins made no secret of his aversion to athletics, famously saying, "Whenever I feel like exercise, I lie down until the feeling passes."[329] He believed that football held entirely too prominent a position at Chicago, and he did not want to be counted among institutions that he contended allocated too many resources to sports, rather than academics.[330]

Unwilling to assume a role that would provide a salary but relegate him to a desk rather than keep him on the field with his boys, Stagg chose to leave the institution he had served for over forty years. The Grand Old Man's exit from Chicago was echoed by the ignominious departure of another coaching legend: Glenn "Pop" Warner resigned his position at Stanford on the same day under mounting criticism of his team's poor performance.[331]

Both men embraced the opportunity for an encore performance; Warner's path led to Philadelphia to coach at Temple University. For Alonzo Stagg, the stage was two thousand miles to the west.

*Right*: Dr. William Raney Harper, first president of the University of Chicago, undated. *University of Chicago Photographic Archive, apf1-03000-051, Special Collections Research Center, University of Chicago Library.*

*Below*: University of Chicago football team, 1892. *Second row, left to right*: Henry Gordon Gale, Andrew R.E. Wyant, George Nelson Knapp, Amos Alonzo Stagg (acting captain, holding football), William Rullkoetter, William Rufus Smith, Charles William Allen, Richard E. Brenneman, John Lemay, John V. Fradenburg. *First row*: William John Rapp, Clifford Bottsford McGillivray, Henry Thurston Chace (on floor), Joseph Edward Raycroft, William B. Conover. *University of Chicago Photographic Archive, apf4-00669, Special Collections Research Center, University of Chicago Library.*

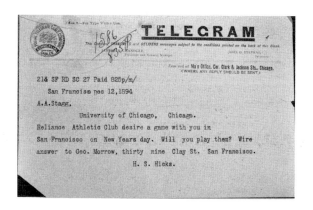

December 5, 1894 telegram from H.S. Hicks of Stanford to Alonzo Stagg at the University of Chicago confirming the teams' game in San Francisco later that month. *Stagg, Amos Alonzo. Papers, Box 18, Folder 6, Special Collections Research Center, University of Chicago Library.*

December 12, 1894 telegram from H.S. Hicks of Stanford advising Alonzo Stagg of Reliance Athletic Club's interest in playing Stagg's Maroons on New Year's Day 1895 in San Francisco. *Stagg, Amos Alonzo. Papers, Box 18, Folder 6, Special Collections Research Center, University of Chicago Library.*

September 1894 wedding of Stella Robertson and Amos Alonzo Stagg. *University of Chicago Photographic Archive, apf1-07768, Special Collections Research Center, University of Chicago Library.*

*Right*: Proud father Amos Alonzo Stagg Sr. with his infant son, Amos Alonzo Stagg Jr., 1899. *University of Chicago Photographic Archive, apf1-07890, Special Collections Research Center, University of Chicago Library.*

*Opposite, top*: University of Chicago football team, 1894. *Fourth row, left to right*: Walter Eugene Garrey, Charles Foster Roby, George Nelson Knapp, Henry Gordon Gale, William Rullkoetter, Frederick Day Nichols, Robert Newton Tooker. *Third row*: Emery Roscoe Yundt, Amos Alonzo Stagg (coach), Charles William Allen (captain), Horace Webster Black. *Second row*: Henry Thurston Chace, Frank Earle Hering. *First row*: John Lemay, Clarence Bert Herschberger. *University of Chicago Photographic Archive, apf4-00672, Special Collections Research Center, University of Chicago Library.*

*Opposite, bottom*: Stella, Alonzo Sr. and Alonzo Stagg Jr., 1899. *Courtesy of the Stagg family collection.*

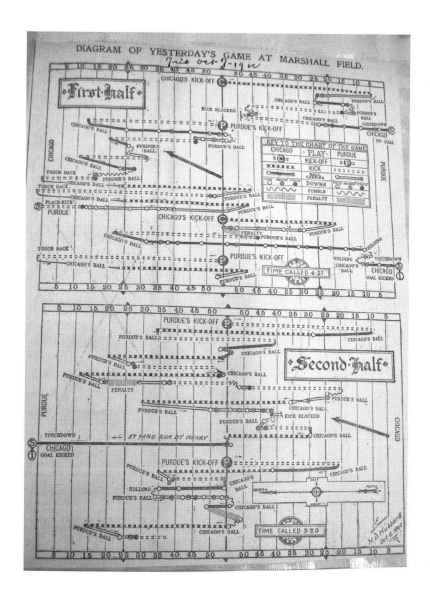

Diagram of the October 6, 1900 game between Chicago and Purdue at Marshall Field. Chicago won, 17–5. *Stagg, Amos Alonzo. Papers, Box 135, Scrapbook 17, Special Collections Research Center, University of Chicago Library.*

*Right*: Hugo F. Bezdek, member of the University of Chicago football team (1902–5) and baseball team (1903–5). He coached at the University of Oregon, the University of Arkansas, Penn State University and Delaware Valley College. Bezdek also coached the Cleveland Rams and managed the Pittsburgh Pirates. *University of Chicago Photographic Archive, apf5-00173, Special Collections Research Center, University of Chicago Library.*

*Below*: Walter Eckersall in action for the Maroons at Marshall Field, circa 1904. *University of Chicago Photographic Archive, apf4-00309, Special Collections Research Center, University of Chicago Library.*

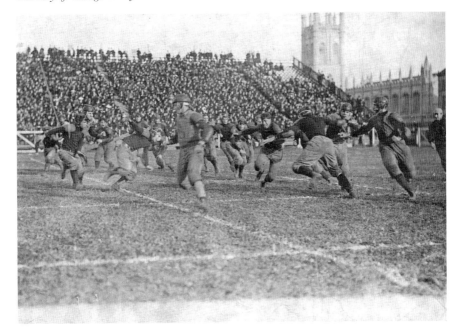

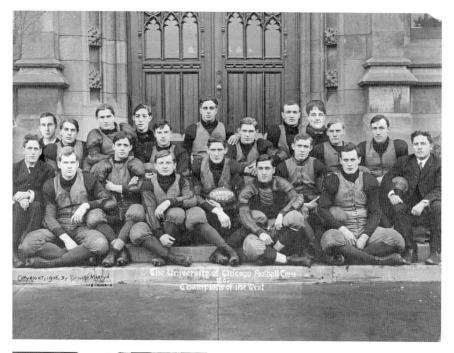

*Above*: University of Chicago football team, 1905, Champions of the West. *Fourth row, from left*: Frederick Adolph Speik (assistant coach), Fred Mitchell Walker, Leo Carter DeTray, Merrill Church Meigs, William James Boone, Melville Archibald Hill. *Third row*: Gerry Williamsen, Lewis Daniel Scherer, Edwin Eugene Parry, Lester LaMont Larson, Clarence Russell. *Second row*: Hiram B. Conibear (trainer), Carl Huntley Hitchcock, Mark Seavey Catlin (captain), Jesse Claire Harper, Amos Alonzo Stagg (coach). *First row*: Arthur Hill Badenoch, Hugo Francis Bezdek, Walter Herbert Eckersall, Burton Pike Gale. *University of Chicago Photographic Archive, apf4-00691, Special Collections Research Center, University of Chicago Library.*

*Left*: Walter H. Eckersall, student athlete at the University of Chicago, circa 1905. Eckersall played on the football and baseball teams for Amos Alonzo Stagg. *University of Chicago Photographic Archive, apf4-00118, Special Collections Research Center, University of Chicago Library.*

*Above*: Walter Steffen at quarterback for the Maroons in their contest with the University of Wisconsin in the final game of the 1908 football season. The game was played at Camp Randall Field in Madison on November 21. Chicago won 18–12. *University of Chicago Photographic Archive, apf4-03825-057, Special Collections Research Center, University of Chicago Library.*

*Left*: Jesse C. Harper, member of the University of Chicago baseball team (1903–6) and football team (1905). During the 1905 season, Harper served as baseball team captain. Harper coached at Alma College, Wabash College and the University of Notre Dame. *University of Chicago Photographic Archive, apf5-00951, Special Collections Research Center, University of Chicago Library.*

Albert A. Michelson, professor and head of the department of physics at the University of Chicago and recipient of the 1907 Nobel Prize in Physics, undated. *University of Chicago Photographic Archive, apf1-04500, Special Collections Research Center, University of Chicago Library.*

Stagg's boys jumping rope as part of their conditioning drills during football practice, undated. *University of Chicago Photographic Archive, apf4-00665, Special Collections Research Center, University of Chicago Library.*

*Above*: Stella Robertson Stagg (*second from right*) and husband Amos Alonzo Stagg are pictured traveling to the 1908 London Olympics on the ship *Philadelphia*. With them are university faculty members Sophonisba Preston Breckinridge (*left*), dean of the College of Arts, Literature and Science and the Samuel Deutsch Professor of Public Welfare Administration; and Marion Talbot (*second from left*), professor of anthropology, head of the department of household administration and dean of women. *University of Chicago Photographic Archive, apf1-07792, Special Collections Research Center, University of Chicago Library.*

*Left*: Harlan "Pat" Page demonstrates a forward pass during practice at the University of Chicago, circa 1908. *University of Chicago Photographic Archive, apf4-03825-060, Special Collections Research Center, University of Chicago Library.*

At the request of his former player Hugo Bezdek, Alonzo Stagg traveled to Fayetteville in March 1910 to teach the forward pass to Coach Bezdek's University of Arkansas football team. While on the Arkansas campus, Stagg and Walter Eckersall experimented with possible changes in the forward pass rule. *University of Chicago Photographic Archive, apf4-00668, Special Collections Research Center, University of Chicago Library.*

Waseda University and the University of Chicago baseball teams at the University of Chicago, circa 1910. *University of Chicago Photographic Archive, apf4-00130, Special Collections Research Center, University of Chicago Library.*

*Above*: Football Rules Committee at the February 3, 1911 session, held in the Hotel Cumberland, New York City. *Standing, from left*: Lieutenant V.W. Cooper, West Point; Dr. H.L. Williams, Minnesota; A.A. Stagg, Chicago; S.C. Williams, Iowa; Lieutenant F.D. Berrien, Annapolis; Professor C.W. Savage, Oberlin; Captain Joseph Beacham, Cornell; Percy Haughton, Harvard. *Sitting*: Dr. Carl Williams, Pennsylvania; Dr. James W. Babbitt, Haverford; Dr. W.L. Dudley, Vanderbilt; E.K. Hall, Dartmouth; Walter Camp, Yale; Parke H. Davis, Princeton. *University of Chicago Photographic Archive, apf4-00667, Special Collections Research Center, University of Chicago Library.*

*Right*: The Stagg family, circa 1911. *Standing, in back*: Alonzo Jr.; *seated, left to right*: Stella, Paul, Alonzo Sr.; *seated, in front*: Ruth. *Courtesy of the Stagg family collection.*

University of Chicago football captain and center Paul "Shorty" Des Jardien (*right*) shakes hands with coach Amos Alonzo Stagg (*left*) after the Chicago Maroons' 34–0 victory over the Indiana Hoosiers on October 3, 1914. Suffering a back injury, Stagg directed his team while seated in a motorcycle sidecar. *University of Chicago Photographic Archive, apf1-07824, Special Collections Research Center, University of Chicago Library.*

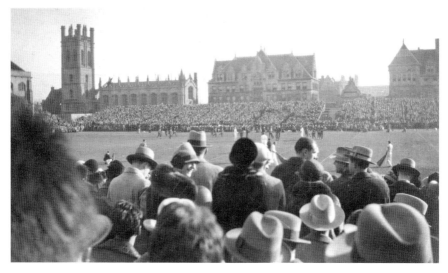

Fans enjoy a game at Stagg Field, undated. *University of Chicago Photographic Archive, apf4-00644, Special Collections Research Center, University of Chicago Library.*

*Left*: Herbert "Fritz" Crisler, member of the University of Chicago football, baseball and basketball teams (1918–21). Crisler won the Big Ten Medal of Honor for football, basketball and baseball in 1922. Crisler coached at the University of Minnesota, Princeton University and the University of Michigan. *University of Chicago Photographic Archive, apf5-00485, Special Collections Research Center, University of Chicago Library.*

*Right*: Milton A. Romney, member of the University of Chicago football team (1921) and basketball team (1922). Romney coached at the University of Texas and played professional football for the Chicago Bears. *University of Chicago Photographic Archive, apf5-01989, Special Collections Research Center, University of Chicago Library.*

Three generations of Staggs: Amos Alonzo Stagg Sr. with his son Amos A. Jr. (*right*) and grandson, Amos A. III (*seated*), circa 1929. *University of Chicago Photographic Archive, apf1-07769, Special Collections Research Center, University of Chicago Library.*

Meeting of football coaches, circa 1930. *From left*: Knute Rockne, University of Notre Dame; Elton "Tad" Wieman, University of Michigan; Glenn Thistlewaite, University of Wisconsin; Amos Alonzo Stagg, University of Chicago; Robert Zuppke, University of Illinois; Harlan O. "Pat" Page, University of Chicago; Richard "Dick" Hanley, Northwestern University; Edward Anderson, DePaul University. *University of Chicago Photographic Archive, apf1-07815, Special Collections Research Center, University of Chicago Library.*

*This page and four following pages*: Stella Stagg's notes from scouting the University of Michigan versus the University of Illinois on October 25, 1930, in Ann Arbor. Chicago played Illinois on November 15 and Michigan on November 22. *Courtesy of the Stagg family collection.*

Orthodox 3 down

**The University of Chicago**
Department of Physical Culture and Athletics
OFFICE OF THE

Went after rumm... Rephysical in 1924-25-28 - not so confident then—

② S

⑩ Michigan lines up very fast + their plays go off with a bang — Any defensive H plays must be acted on instantly to be effective.

⑪ They played 1 play
20 or 25 times — with
pep and determination
as if the game depended
on this play

F T C C G T F
× × ×× O × × ×

Ill defense

× × × ×

Michigan
Punting play

⑫ Michigan's kicking was superb—
The average of 35 yards did not represent
the actual distance in that serial of the
Michigan kicks went out of bounds on Ills
5, 10 or 15 yard line keeping Illinois
in the hole continuously 2/3 of the game.
Ill safety man didn't catch many— those
that went up the field were very high +
the ball twice came down with a short
up Ill Safety man very fumbled—

⑬ Tricks — Old 83 — lead up to cleverly—
played on 3rd down + the fake place kick
played an important part of Michigan's scoring
punch —

⑭ In preparing defense Michigan's superior
speed of men, versatility in technique (curves
cleverness of receivers) must not be underestimated
by the boys — Only superior effort on the

The way Michigan scored on Illinois
Michigan received break when Bury dropped punt Mich recovered in scoring territory

Recovered too late

Wheeler not Michigan territory 70

5

entire

very wide

15

8

5

H

?

C

F

H

E T G G G T E

× ×× O ×× × ×

×

×

×

Wheeler ran over goal line untouched.
Play timed perfectly
All men left immediately
ran very fast — received
on the dead run.
Played on 3rd down
7 to go —

The execution was similar
to those of Dartmouth 1925

③

Michigan received a second break when
they recovered Ills fumble — & tried this play

Goal line

Intercepted by Bury

Recoy

This play
looked like
a sure touch-
down but
Tackled here the
Illinois safety
man made
a remarkable
recovery & timed
his catch perfectly
picking it out of
the air —

I do not believe he would possibly
have covered it if a pass had not
scored — thrown to this spot only 3 minutes
before

Ill H backs
out run
Ill safety man had
tough place —

Michigan took advantage of a 3rd break in
blocking Bodemans punt. Mich used blocking formation

Goal line     New Variety   Old 8 34

Hextra wide

Tried on 3rd down about 4 to go     Mich blocking
I don't believe it would have           formation
worked

Hands
Changed & watd

fumbled

**The University of Chicago**
Department of Physical Culture and Athletics

30  Ranout of bounds

95

Michigan pass that lead up to 2nd touchdown

50

45        very fast runner

40   H        S            H

5

useless
C        F

E   T                T   E

×   × × O × ×        ×
  ×              × ×

        ×

Perfectly timed
perfectly thrown
perfectly received

Open
also        S                    Absolutely free
H                    H
C        Johnny to Ways 48

F  T  × × O × ×  Bartel    T    E
  ×              × ×

Outside of it
being a fake
place kick - I
believe the play
would have
worked - The
execution was
perfect.

*Above*: Reunion in 1929 of the 1899 University of Chicago championship football team. *First row, left to right*: William Eldridge, Dr. Ralph Hamill (captain), Walter S. Kennedy, Jonathan Webb, James Sheldon. *Second row*: A.A. Stagg, J. Wellington, Fred Slaker, Charles G. Flanagan, Kellogg Speed, James Henry, H.F. Ahlswede, E.W. Place. *Third row*: Dr. A.B. Snider, James Garfield MacNab, Bert Cassels, Edward Rich. *University of Chicago Photographic Archive, apf4-00676, Special Collections Research Center, University of Chicago Library.*

*Left*: Paul Stagg, member of the University of Chicago tennis team (1930–32). During the 1932 season, Stagg served as tennis team captain. *University of Chicago Photographic Archive, apf5-02255, Special Collections Research Center, University of Chicago Library.*

Paul Stagg, member of the University of Chicago football team (1929–31).
*University of Chicago Photographic Archive, apf5-02259, Special Collections Research Center,*
*University of Chicago Library.*

*Above*: University of Chicago hosts Stagg's alma mater, Yale University, on October 17, 1931. Yale won, 27–0. *University of Chicago Photographic Archive, apf4-00345, Special Collections Research Center, University of Chicago Library.*

*Left*: Jay Berwanger, University of Chicago halfback (1933–35), member of the 1935 All-America team and winner of the first Heisman Trophy. During his three years at Chicago, Berwanger gained 4,108 yards. *University of Chicago Photographic Archive, apf4-00641, Special Collections Research Center, University of Chicago Library.*

## Chapter 17

# WESTWARD BOUND

**T**hree weeks after his seventy-first birthday, Alonzo and Stella Stagg moved to Stockton, California, where the Grand Old Man set about the business of building a football team from among a student body of just over eight hundred co-eds.[332] When Stagg arrived at the College of the Pacific, *Central Press* sports editor William Ritt welcomed his advent with muted optimism.

"Only a miracle could create in Pacific another Centre College."[333] (The small Danville, Kentucky school amassed a 57-8 record from 1917 to 1924, competing against the nation's top football programs and defeating the likes of Harvard, TCU, Alabama and Ole Miss.)[334] But Ritt went on to add that Stagg's decision to lead a program without a strong football reputation was a great thing for the sport.

Stagg's transformation of the Pacific Tigers during his fourteen-year tenure could be described as miraculous, and without a doubt, college football benefited from the team's success. Under Stagg's leadership, the Tigers challenged powerhouse programs of the West Coast—always putting up a strong fight and often emerging victorious. Ever a champion for the little guy, Stagg answered his critics simply: "Well, if you don't schedule the big fellow, how can you ever expect to defeat him?"[335]

In Stagg's second year, Pacific opened its season against USC at the Coliseum. The Tigers held the Trojans to a single touchdown late in the third quarter on a drive that began when a penalty against Pacific gave the ball back to USC on the Tigers' seventeen-yard line. Midway through the third period, a Trojan drive stalled at midfield. During the ensuing punt, Tiger safety Jim Bainbridge fell to the ground blocking a USC tackler. While he lay on the field, the punt grazed his ankle and, as a result, was a live ball when downed by USC end Jed Ostling. The Trojans capitalized on the momentum generated by the ball's inadvertent bounce and scored the game's only touchdown.

A crowd of thirty-five thousand witnessed the quick-tempo, wide-open battle that kept fans on their feet with their hearts racing. Owing to the thrill—and perhaps the ninety-six-degree Los Angeles heat—two women fainted and had to be carried from the stands, prompting one reporter to comment, "They were probably wives of the Trojan coaching staff."[336] The highly favored home team narrowly escaped with a 6–0 victory, having been put on notice that the Davids of Stockton would not cower before any Goliath in the West.

In November 1938, Stagg returned to the Midway for the Tigers' first and only contest with the Maroons. Normally a grandstand fixture with her notebook full of charts, Stella instead remained on the West Coast to scout Chico State, the Tigers' opponent the following week.[337] The Grand Old Man received a hero's welcome from the crowd of some ten thousand gathered for his Stagg Field homecoming, and at halftime, the Order of the C presented him with a scroll proclaiming, "All-time All-America Coach." In the game's final minutes, the Tigers thwarted the Maroons' only scoring threat when Pacific's Bobby Kientz intercepted Sollie Sherman's pass at the goal line and ran ninety-nine yards for a touchdown.[338] The crowd that set out the welcome mat for Stagg was no doubt happy to see his Tigers leave following their 32–0 victory.

Stagg's gridiron squad continued to challenge the titans of the West under his leadership in the 1930s and '40s. In 1943, Pacific defeated St. Mary's Pre-Flight, UCLA and California en route to a final ranking of nineteen in the AP poll, and the eighty-one-year-old was named Coach of the Year by the American Football Coaches Association.

Stagg's tenure at College of the Pacific came to an end in December 1946, when he declined the school's offer to move from the sidelines into the role of "consultant in athletics." During his final season as their head coach, Stagg led the Tigers to a disappointing 3-7 record, including a heart-breaking one-point loss to the North Texas State Mean Green in the Optimist Bowl.[339]

For the eighty-four-year-old coach, a losing season did not signal the end of a career, however. Stagg explained his position to Chancellor Tully Knoles, echoing his sentiments of fourteen years earlier when he had left Chicago for Stockton: "I am fully convinced that the pearl of great price for me is to continue my life's purpose of helping young men through the relationship of coaching. That was the reason I did not accept the proposal to remain at the University of Chicago at a large salary."[340]

The wisdom of Stagg's words would be borne out in the success of two young men of Pacific, in particular.

## Chapter 18

# THE MIGHTY TIGERS

G o ask her." The offensive linemen pressed Hardin as the coach's whistle signaled an end to the day's practice. "You gotta ask her what she's doing."

Hardin, the youngest member of the squad, reluctantly complied. His teammates' seniority gave them the authority, and he knew it was pointless to argue.

He jogged from midfield to the sideline seat of the petite woman holding a notebook filled with drawings and handwritten notes. "Excuse me, Mrs. Stagg. The guys and I noticed you sitting over here. Mind if I ask what you're doing?"

Stella Stagg looked up from her work. "Young man," she said matter-of-factly, "I'm just deciding whether you start on Saturday or not."

Three days later, the Tigers faced off against the St. Mary's Navy Pre-Flight Airdevils. By a 14–6 margin, Pacific outmanned a highly favored St. Mary's team that would go on to dominate Cal and UCLA later in the season. But in that September 1944 contest, the Navy gridders had no answer for a pair of freshmen who manned the backfield in the Tigers' assault. One was a 180-pound fullback, the other a fleet-footed wingback key to Stagg's man-in-motion scheme named Wayne Hardin.[341]

Hardin started every game of the 1944 regular season until his required enlistment into military service prevented him from playing late-season contests against the San Francisco Coast Guard Pilots and the UCLA Bruins. By late October, Stagg had lost over half his team to the wartime-mandated transfers that relocated marine and navy trainees to other institutions for advanced military courses.[342]

The depleted Pacific squad fought hard against the Pilots but finished on the losing end of a 13–0 score.[343] UCLA, however, ran with impunity against the outmatched Tigers. Under the leadership of backfield coach Bronko Nagurski, the Bruin rushers gained 330 yards. The University of Minnesota and Chicago Bears great coached just one year; unfortunately for the Staggmen, that year was 1944, and nine of their eleven starters were unavailable for the encounter with Nagurski and his backfield. Pacific needed the swift young Wayne Hardin and his ten fellow first-stringers all playing the game of their lives to overcome the Bruins' punishing ground and air attack. As it was, the outmanned Tigers' shortened season ended with a 54–7 loss to UCLA.[344]

Hardin fulfilled his commitment to the military and returned to Stockton and a promising college career. During his tenure at Pacific, Hardin served as a utility man, playing halfback, quarterback, safety and kicker for the Tigers.

Despite their sixty-year age difference, Stagg and Hardin developed a close bond. Early in his career as a high school and junior college coach, Hardin leaned heavily on lessons he learned in Stagg's classroom. "He used to demonstrate the things he wanted done," said Hardin, recalling his coach's practice of running through plays on the field with his team. "The techniques he used then are sound today."[345]

After graduating from Pacific, Hardin embarked on a coaching career that spanned more than thirty years, compiling an NCAA Division I head coaching record of 118-74-5.[346] He mentored some of college football's greatest players, including the U.S. Naval Academy's only Heisman Award winners: Joe Bellino and Roger Staubach.

In 1959, Coach Hardin took the reins at Navy, and the Black Knights of Army also welcomed a new head coach. As Hardin succeeded Eddie Erdelatz, who left his post under protest over Navy's athletic department policies,[347] Dale Hall followed Earl Blaik, the legendary Army coach of three national championship teams and three Heisman Trophy winners.[348]

Hardin's innovative ideas raised more than a few eyebrows among the Navy faithful during his first season as the head man. He paved uncharted ground by exchanging game film with Army's head coach prior to the service academies' contest in 1959. It was a practice Army's Red Blaik had long objected to, believing that Navy had no business seeing film of his team at practice. Hardin, however, took a pragmatic view of the matter: "Hall and I figured it was better to exchange our films freely than to slip around the back door trying to get them elsewhere."[349] Stella Stagg, no doubt, would have approved.

As the season opened, Hardin was reminded of the Staggs' lessons on scouting opponents when his team faced off against Boston College. Navy's athletic department had no film on his first opponent as Hardin prepared for his debut as the leader on the Navy sidelines. The Midshipmen defeated the Eagles in Chestnut Hill, but not before the home team ran several plays that took Hardin and company by surprise. In a post-game interview, Hardin coyly acknowledged the missteps and hinted that his men would be better prepared for their upcoming contest with William and Mary. "Being able to scout the other team is a big help," he said.[350]

The following week, the Midshipmen and a crowd of Navy faithful celebrated the dedication of the new Navy–Marine Corps Memorial Stadium with a 29–2 victory over a well-scouted William and Mary Indians team.[351]

Like the Grand Old Man, Hardin embraced innovation on the gridiron. In his first year at Navy, Hardin introduced a twenty-two-man first team distinct from the two-platoon system of offensive and defensive specialists that had become commonplace throughout the college thanks to Fritz Crisler. Beginning with Hardin's first game as head coach, the Midshipmen fielded two complete eleven-man teams of equal ability. Each squad played both ways—for roughly seven-and-a-half-minute intervals. In a preseason interview, Hardin explained his rationale. "Because of the vigorous training program all Midshipmen go through, we feel we're in better physical shape than many teams and can benefit by using separate units. The substituting rule has been changed some for the 1959 season and under it, we will be able to send units in and out more easily."[352] Hardin employed his strategy with successful results against Boston College and, when asked about the makeup of each squad, explained, "We're just using our personnel the best way we know how to win."[353]

By his fourth season at Navy, Hardin had made more sweeping changes to his lineup, at one point fielding a team with only one senior in a starting role. One of the underclassmen starting on the offense was sophomore quarterback Roger Staubach. Hardin promoted Staubach when senior Ron Klenick struggled to lead the offense early in the season. Staubach handled snaps from junior center Tom Lynch. The future rear admiral and superintendent of the Naval Academy was also promoted into a starting role following a rocky start to the 1962 campaign.[354]

In his first start, Staubach went 0 for 2 passing and was sacked twice for -24 yards en route to a 21–0 pounding by the University of Minnesota.[355]

Coach Hardin maintained his bullish view of Staubach's potential, nevertheless. A week after Navy's loss to the Golden Gophers at the Brickhouse, Staubach was near-perfect, going 9 for 11, scoring one touchdown through the air and two on the ground, in a 41–0 defeat of Cornell.[356] At the end of his sophomore season, Staubach led the NCAA with a 67.3 percent pass completion rate. More importantly, his four touchdowns in the season's final game propelled Navy to a 34–14 victory over Army.[357]

As a junior, Staubach led the Midshipmen to a 9-1 record, including a 35–14 win over Notre Dame, a feat that would not be repeated for forty-three years.[358] *Time* and *Sports Illustrated* showcased him on their covers.[359] And in December 1963, Staubach, whose ignominious first start a season earlier cast doubts on his head coach's judgment, became Wayne Hardin's and Navy's second quarterback to win the Heisman Trophy.[360]

Hardin understood the coach's role. While many of his coaching contemporaries deflected praise directed toward themselves, Hardin lamented his peers' inclination toward modesty. He believed instead in the honest reporting of a coach's merits. "The days of men like [Knute] Rockne, Stagg, and [Fritz] Crisler are gone," said Hardin. "These men would go out and sell themselves and sell their professions and the public loved it. Coaches [today] are afraid to admit that they are doing a good job because of their own inborn and acquired talents. If a man has a successful season record-wise, he says it's because of the team's talent, or because the students or the town were behind him. But he never says 'it's because I did a good job in training and teaching those boys; that I helped mold them into a team, and that I spent grueling hours over films and charts, and on the practice field, working like a dog.'"[361]

***

In Alonzo Stagg's final season at Pacific, a five-foot, seven-inch, 155-pound, sixteen-year-old freshman arrived on campus eager to play quarterback for the Tigers. By November, Eddie LeBaron had earned the job and the first of his four varsity letters. Like he had done four decades earlier with the 145-pound Walter Eckersall, Stagg took a young, undersized player and fashioned a champion. And as LeBaron fondly recalled, age never minimized the Grand Old Man's enthusiasm. "We were in Chicago for a game with Northwestern, and the players were just milling around the hotel lobby. Mr.

Stagg walked in and blew his whistle to signal it was time to go. There were a few older ladies sitting in the lobby at the same time, and I think it took them a few minutes to regain their composure."[362]

A week earlier, the team learned that age also did not moderate Stagg's insistence on adhering to the rules. En route to their date with Northwestern in Chicago, the Tigers traveled to Tucson to play the University of Arizona. As the train approached a stop in Los Angeles, Stagg saw one of his players smoking a cigarette. With no fanfare or even discussion, Stagg handed him ten dollars and told him to take the train back to Stockton.[363]

The Tigers arrived at Dyche Stadium to face Northwestern, and from the opening kick, Stagg paced the sidelines as he watched the unrelenting power of the Wildcat backs. Early in the first quarter, Wayne Hardin missed a high tackle on Northwestern's Ken Wiltgen. Stagg immediately pulled him from the field.

"You're making us look bad with those necktie tackles, son. Hit 'em low," the coach admonished.

Later in the first half, Hardin broke off a seventy-yard touchdown run following a spectacular interception and double lateral. Following the play, the Grand Old Man again pulled Hardin from the field.

"You're making us look good now, son. But remember, hit 'em low!"[364]

During the halftime ceremony, a crowd of thirty-five thousand welcomed Stagg's return to Chicago with a standing ovation. Western conference commissioner Tug Wilson praised Stagg's efforts in helping to establish the Big Ten more than half a century earlier. The festivities continued with a keynote address by the game's umpire, John Schommer, star of Stagg's 1908 squad and inaugural member of the Jackass Club.

As he concluded his remarks, Schommer turned to Ted Payseur, Northwestern's athletic director, and said, "Speaking for the Order of the 'C,' and all the friends of Mr. Stagg, I wish Northwestern the best of luck in the future—but not in the second half."[365]

The Tigers lost to the number-eight-ranked Wildcats, 26–13, but LeBaron provided some late-game excitement with a touchdown pass to Ed Waits following a Northwestern fumble.

LeBaron and Hardin supplied the spark in an otherwise lackluster 1946 season for the Tigers as they led Pacific to a 31–6 defeat of the University of California–Davis Aggies and an invitation to play in the December 21 Optimist Bowl game.[366]

LeBaron started as quarterback, safety and punter for the next three years and earned All-America honors in 1949 as he led the Tigers to an undefeated season and ranking of ten in the final AP poll.[367] When he graduated in the spring of 1950, LeBaron was drafted by the NFL's Washington Redskins, but the outbreak of war in Korea propelled him into active duty with the Marine Corps. He served with distinction in Korea, earning the Purple Heart and Bronze Star. Following his discharge in 1952, he returned to the Redskins and played backup to Sammy Baugh. The two men shared the quarterback duties, and LeBaron's play earned him a spot on the NFL's All-Rookie Team as well as the starting role when the legendary Baugh retired at the end of the season.

"The Little General," as he came to be known, enjoyed great success with the Redskins, as a three-time Pro Bowl selection and as the NFL's passing leader in 1958. He also attended George Washington University law school in the offseason, graduating sixth in his class in 1959.[368] When LeBaron left the Redskins in 1959, he planned to hang up his cleats and begin working with a Midland, Texas law firm. A new NFL franchise obtained rights to him, however, and offered him a $20,000-per-year contract. So instead of settling into an office in west Texas, LeBaron began work as the first quarterback of the Dallas Cowboys.[369]

In 2006, the University of the Pacific athletics department presented LeBaron with the Amos Alonzo Stagg Award of Honor, which "recognizes alumni who participated in athletics at Pacific and achieved distinction in their professional lives through the notable examples of integrity, dedication, idealism, and team spirit that Mr. Stagg personified and to which Pacific is dedicated."[370] During the ceremony, the 1947 team was inducted into the University of the Pacific Athletic Hall of Fame. Wayne Hardin was inducted individually in 1998.

At the close of the 1946 season at Pacific, an eighty-four-year-old Alonzo Stagg was forced into a second unwanted retirement. The fortunes of college football's 1944 Coach of the Year had changed, and the Grand Old Man of Football found himself starting a new job for only the second time in fifty-five years. Still not ready to accept a position that consigned him merely to consulting an athletic program, Stagg moved east to join his son Alonzo Jr. on the sidelines of a small Lutheran school in rural Pennsylvania.

*Chapter 19*

# THE STAGGS AT SUSQUEHANNA

I n 1935, Alonzo Stagg Jr. accepted the head coaching job at Susquehanna University in Selinsgrove, Pennsylvania, about fifty miles north of Harrisburg. After a little more than a decade at the helm, Stagg Jr. continued to experience inconsistent results with his gridiron squads. In 1947, he welcomed the addition of his father to the team, hopeful the coaching legend's assistance would lead to success against opponents such as Allegheny and Haverford. News outlets reported that Susquehanna's administration expressed its confidence in the hiring decision—and the Grand Old Man's stamina—by offering him a ten-year contract.[371] When asked to confirm the report's accuracy, the elder Stagg simply said, "I am not big enough to challenge the Almighty. And that would be a challenge. I'll keep working as long as He lets me—and I hope that will be a long, long time."[372]

At Susquehanna, the Staggs established a division of coaching labor such that Alonzo Sr. took charge of the offense and Alonzo Jr. led the defense. As she had done at Chicago and Pacific, Stella served as the team's scout. And when called upon, she willingly served as a blocking back for her husband as he demonstrated new plays in the Staggs' backyard.[373]

Stella's command of the game's details left little room to doubt her judgments, and the uniqueness of her expertise garnered the attention of a media captivated by an octogenarian football coach.

Soon after arriving in Selinsgrove, the Staggs were interviewed by a reporter with the *American Weekly*. They walked across the picturesque

Susquehanna campus, taking in the fall beauty with the visiting reporter. At one point, Mr. Stagg froze at attention at the sound of a football being kicked into the October air. A second sound followed, and he declared the unseen kick to have traveled fifty yards. With her own finely calibrated ear for football, Stella responded, "Don't be so sure, Alonzo. There's a stiff wind today. It might have gone straight up." She winked as her husband of fifty-three years broke out in a laugh and told the reporter, "That's the only thing we disagree on!"[374]

As the men of Susquehanna prepared to play Dickinson in October 1947, Stella's scouting report included an observation that "their left defensive halfback comes up quickly on pass plays." Her advice to the Grand Old Man that "we can throw beyond him" was spot-on, as the Crusaders scored on a pass over the head of the Red Devils' defensive halfback.[375] Unfortunately, Dickinson bested Susquehanna, 33–27, in a battle that included four total touchdowns in the game's final quarter.[376] But on the strength of Stella's scouting, the Crusaders would not lose another game the rest of the season.[377]

Susquehanna again struggled with inconsistent play through the 1948 and 1949 seasons. The team began a turnaround in 1950, and in 1951, the Staggs coached the men of Susquehanna to an undefeated and untied season.[378] The opening contest of the six-game campaign provided the only threat of defeat, as the Crusaders beat Johns Hopkins, 34–32, with time expiring.[379]

Following Susquehanna's perfect 1951 season, center James Hazlett was named to the Associated Press's little college All-America team. Hazlett chose to forego offers from larger and more prominent schools for the opportunity to play for the legendary Stagg. The senior Stagg, despite being named to Walter Camp's first All-America team, never named one of his own players to an all-star team; however, he did not hesitate to declare his center's value to the squad: "Just say that without Jim Hazlett, Susquehanna would not have enjoyed the success it did this year."[380] Susquehanna's three-sport star Hazlett returned to his alma mater in 1966 as athletic director and coach of the football and baseball teams. His 1970 football squad won the 1970 MAC Northern Division title.[381]

As Hazlett was being feted with All-America accolades and the Crusaders reveled in the glories of their 1951 campaign, eighty-nine-year-old Alonzo Stagg continued to make headlines. In December, the celebrated coach became the subject of rumors among professional football writers who speculated that he would be named head coach of the Chicago Cardinals—filling the vacancy created by the departure of E.L. "Curly" Lambeau. Fueling the speculation was Stagg's trip to Chicago in early December; however, a source close to the coaching legend attempted to quash the rumors by telling the *Chicago Tribune*, "Stagg is not interested in making a change. He will not take the Cardinal job."[382] History would note the only relationship between Alonzo Stagg and the Chicago Cardinals was when, in 1901, the team's owner, Chris O'Brien, purchased used football jerseys from the nearby University of Chicago. The well-worn jerseys were a faded maroon, which prompted O'Brien to declare, "That's not maroon, it's Cardinal red!"[383] The name was born, and although the team later relocated to St. Louis and then to Arizona, the franchise's name remained unchanged.

Despite overtures from other organizations, Alonzo Sr. coached alongside Alonzo Jr. at Susquehanna through 1953. He and Stella lived with their son and family during the football season and returned to their home in Stockton the remainder of the year.

During the Staggs' years in Selinsgrove, Stella continued her practice of chronicling the games with detailed notes and diagrams. She was usually accompanied by Ruth Eleanor McCorkill, who, in 1943, had become Susquehanna's first female sports information director.[384] When the Crusaders played away games, the two women rode the team bus along with the players and coaches. During this era, women were not allowed in the press box of many college stadiums, so Stella and Ruth Eleanor recorded statistics and captured the games' highlights from the bleachers at Swarthmore, Allegheny and the like. Back home at Susquehanna, though, the women found a warm welcome in the press box, where all of the occupants knew Mrs. Stagg was as fluent in the game as any coach on the field—her husband included.[385]

McCorkill developed a close relationship with the Staggs during their years at Susquehanna and spent several weeks with them at their Stockton home in the summer. During her first visit, McCorkill's hosts invited her to enjoy the swimming pool, and she confessed that she did not know how to swim. Determined to remedy the situation, Alonzo Stagg told Ruth Eleanor to jump into the pool. The coach, at nearly ninety years old, proceeded to walk along the side while simultaneously explaining and demonstrating various strokes until his young pupil had mastered each one.[386] "He never stopped teaching," Ruth Eleanor declared, "and he wouldn't accept anything less than full effort from his students."

\*\*\*

Beginning in the mid-1940s, several leading motion picture producers began courting Mr. Stagg in hopes of securing the rights to his life story. Metro Goldwyn Meyer even sent a representative to Selinsgrove in 1948 to make a personal appeal, but Alonzo Stagg insisted he was not interested. As his sixtieth year of coaching football dawned, Stagg was busily preparing for Susquehanna's upcoming contest with Wagner and had no time for watching motion pictures—and certainly not for helping to develop a screenplay about his life. MGM Studios went so far as to engage Spencer Tracy and Katharine Hepburn to star in the proposed film, but Stagg maintained his refusal. Years later, Alonzo Stagg Jr. described his father's response to the studio executives' repeated requests.

> *Coach Stagg was motivated very much by a desire to serve his Maker. He was a perfectionist—he had a motive of serving young men. He had very little interest in money. At Susquehanna, my father was approached by MGM to make a story of his life; they followed him and worked on him. They sold me. My father hesitated and gave them no promise. I said "Father—you have a chance to spread your life, your ideals, to millions of people. It is not about money."*
>
> *Out of clear blue one day, he said, "If I were to receive $300,000 or 7% of the gross (about $1 million) from making the picture, I would give it to Yale. Perhaps some to Chicago. But I most certainly wouldn't give it to the children."*

Stagg Sr.'s refusal to gift his children with the proceeds of his life story was not motivated by selfishness or greed. Rather, he considered profiting from one's good name to be an "odious" practice. "He didn't do it by principle," stated Alonzo Jr., "and so it didn't happen."[387]

\*\*\*

Alonzo Stagg's third retirement from coaching came of his own initiative. As Stella's health began to deteriorate, Coach Stagg heeded the advice of doctors and remained in Stockton rather than returning to the Northeast to coach college football for a sixty-fourth year.

"My buddy, the mainstay and center of my life for 59 years, needs me. I will stay by her in every way," he declared in August 1953 as he tendered his resignation at Susquehanna.[388]

The University of Chicago versus College of the Pacific at Stagg Field, November 12, 1938. *University of Chicago Photographic Archive, apf4-00439. Special Collections Research Center, University of Chicago Library.*

College of the Pacific
Opening Day of Practice, September 8-1942.

Alonzo Stagg leads his team onto the field on the opening day of practice at College of the Pacific, September 8, 1942. He is eighty years old. *Courtesy of the Stagg family collection.*

AMOS ALONZO STAGG
127 WEST EUCLID AVENUE
STOCKTON, CALIFORNIA

July 5, 1955

Coach Wayne Hardin
Porterville, California

Dear Wayne:

Mrs. Stagg joins me in congratulations
to you on your fine appointment to be one of
the coaches for the U.S. Navy football team
at Annapolis. I am enclosing the announcement
made in the Stockton Record.

Good luck to you and lots of good
wishes.

with affectionate remembrances,

Amos Alonzo Stagg

July 5, 1955 letter from Alonzo Stagg to former player Wayne Hardin following Hardin's appointment to the coaching staff of the U.S. Naval Academy. *Courtesy of the Stagg family collection.*

Cast members of *Knute Rockne: All-American*, the 1940 film about the legendary Notre Dame football coach, on location at the University of Notre Dame in South Bend, Indiana. *From left*: Henry O'Neill (doctor); Pat O'Brien (Knute Rockne); Stella Robertson Stagg; Nick Lukats (technical advisor and member of the Four Horseman backfield); Amos Alonzo Stagg. Mr. Stagg appeared as himself in the film. *University of Chicago Photographic Archive, apf1-007801, Special Collections Research Center, University of Chicago Library.*

The father-son coaching duo relax after football practice at Susquehanna University, undated. *Courtesy of Susquehanna University archives.*

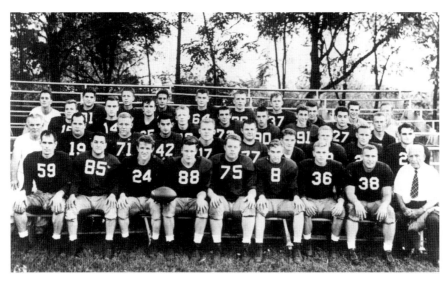

Undefeated and untied Susquehanna University football team of 1951 with co-coaches Amos Alonzo Stagg (*right, first row*) and Amos Alonzo Stagg Jr. (*left, second row*). *University of Chicago Photographic Archive, apf1-11152, Special Collections Research Center, University of Chicago Library.*

Alonzo Stagg pictured with certificates noting his induction into the National Football Hall of Fame as both player (Yale) and coach (University of Chicago, University of the Pacific and Susquehanna University). Stagg is a member of the inaugural class (1951) and was the first man to be inducted as both a player and a coach. *University of Chicago Photographic Archive, apf1-07867 Special Collections Research Center, University of Chicago Library.*

Alonzo Stagg leads his team in a warm-up run around the football field at Susquehanna University, September 3, 1952. He is ninety years old. *Courtesy of the Stagg family collection. Credit: United Press Photo.*

*Right*: Stella Stagg takes notes and charts plays during a Susquehanna University football game, undated. *Courtesy of Susquehanna University archives.*

*Below*: May 14, 1954 luncheon at the Biltmore Hotel in Los Angeles to honor Amos Alonzo Stagg (*second from left, standing*). He is pictured with former Chicago football players (*second row, from right*) Saul C. Weislow, Paul "Shorty" Des Jardien, Edward Parry, John Vruwink; (*first row*) Norman C. "Red" Paine, John Moulds, Mr. Stagg, Norman Barker, Anatol "Speed" Raysson (*seated*). *University of Chicago Photographic Archive, apf1-07840 Special Collections Research Center, University of Chicago Library.*

Four generations of Staggs, undated. *Standing, left to right*: Amos Alonzo III, Amos Alonzo
Sr., Amos Alonzo Jr. *Seated*: Amos Alonzo IV, Stella Stagg, undated. *University of Chicago
Photographic Archive, apf1-07764, Special Collections Research Center, University of Chicago Library.*

Amos Alonzo Stagg speaks at a student awards dinner on June 3, 1955, during the University of Chicago alumni reunion. *University of Chicago Photographic Archive, apf1-07831 Special Collections Research Center, University of Chicago Library.*

Major League Baseball Hall of Famer Jackie Robinson (1919–1972) speaks at Springfield College in 1962 to celebrate Amos Alonzo Stagg's 100th birthday. Hanging behind Robinson are a portrait of Mr. Stagg and the official seal of the Phillips Exeter Academy. *Courtesy of Springfield College, Babson Library, Archives and Special Collections.*

Jay Berwanger, University of Chicago halfback (1933–35) and winner of the first Heisman Trophy in 1935. Berwanger is pictured here, in 1978, at the ceremony where he donated the award to the university; the first Heisman Trophy is displayed in the Berwanger Trophy Room of Bartlett Gymnasium. *University of Chicago Photographic Archive, apf4-00647 Special Collections Research Center, University of Chicago Library.*

Former players gather to honor Amos Alonzo Stagg at the 2014 dedication of the statue honoring the legendary coach and his son Amos Alonzo Stagg Jr. at Susquehanna University. *Courtesy of Susquehanna University Archives.*

Coach Wayne Hardin holding the Stagg Hat Trophy at Susquehanna University in 2016. The trophy is awarded to the winner of the annual football game between Susquehanna and Lycoming College. *Courtesy of author's personal collection.*

*Chapter 20*

# RETURN TO STOCKTON

The prospect of a college football landscape without the Grand Old Man walking one of its sidelines prompted many of his former players to reflect on their enduring affection for their coach. George Varnell, the *Seattle Times* sports editor who played for Stagg at Chicago, recalled a recent visit with his coach.

"Mr. Stagg—and incidentally, he's 'Mr. Stagg' to all his boys—came to Seattle, and some of us—his former players—got together at a luncheon for him. When the waitress came to our table the Old Man ordered lunch for each of us without asking one of us what we wanted. And, do you know, we didn't resent it a bit. We'll always be 'his boys,' and he'll always think he knows what is best for us. We won't argue with him either."[389]

Stagg remained retired for almost a month.

With Stella's blessing, the ninety-one-year-old returned to the gridiron at the request of his former pupil Earl Klapstein. Stockton College's head coach, who starred on Stagg's 1943 Pacific Tigers' team, hired his mentor as the quarterbacks' and punters' coach.

During practice, Stagg joined his players on the field, as had been his custom for the previous six decades. In mid-September 1954, the start of his second year at Stockton, Stagg was on the sidelines as the offense ran through drills. The team's center, with the enthusiasm of a man trying to earn a starting spot, ran his blocking route right into the unsuspecting coach. Coach Klapstein immediately called for an ambulance to take the unconscious Stagg to the hospital for treatment. Before emergency personnel arrived, however, the ninety-two-year-old was alert and back on his feet.

"You don't have to worry about me," Stagg reassured the players and coaches gathered around him. "I know how to take care of myself." He blew his whistle and drilled his squad for another ninety minutes.[390]

The following June, Lon and Stella returned to the University of Chicago to commemorate the fiftieth anniversary of the school's 1905 national championship football team. During the festivities on the Midway, the Old Man threw out the first pitch in the annual alumni-varsity baseball game. At the dinner for the Order of the "C," he greeted his former players by name and reminisced with captain Mark Catlin and Art Badenoch about the epic 2–0 defeat of Michigan. At the celebration's climax, Stagg delivered the evening's address and beamed with delight when Stella was presented with a "C"—the first woman so honored.[391]

In 1958, Stagg received the proceeds of an insurance policy he had taken out in 1892—beating statistical odds of 100,000 to 3 for life expectancy.[392] The man who witnessed the presidencies of both Abraham Lincoln and John F. Kennedy proved such an actuarial anomaly that New York Life issued him the check for $690 on his ninety-sixth birthday. Naturally, he and Stella celebrated the achievement by attending a football game—a charity game in his honor played by Lodi, California high schools.[393]

Two years later, Stagg tendered his resignation to Stockton College and to the great game. "It was a lot of fun and I have no regrets," he declared. "I taught a lot of boys something."[394]

A fall at age ninety-nine, coupled with failing eyesight, forced Coach Stagg's move into a nursing home in February 1963. But in August, with his trademark grit and the aid of his "best assistant," he joined a crowd of nearly four hundred, including California governor Edmund Brown, assembled in Stockton to celebrate his 100th birthday.[395]

In the week that followed, hundreds of former players joined friends and family members in a dozen celebrations from New Jersey to California to mark the occasion.[396] Nearly as many sent letters and telegrams from all over the world. They all joined the National Football Foundation and Hall of Fame in honoring Amos Alonzo Stagg as "the game's greatest teacher." At the Naval Academy Club, several of Stagg's boys, including Wayne Hardin, gathered with a Washington-area crowd to celebrate the milestone. Those who had recently visited with their beloved mentor encouraged Hardin to travel to Stockton to see Mr. Stagg.[397]

Eleven months later, on July 22, 1964, Alonzo Stagg's "best assistant" died at age eighty-eight.[398] "Mother did a tremendous amount of work to help my father," said Alonzo Jr. following Stella's death. "She viewed it as her responsibility to help him. She was completely self-sacrificing. She could work, and she did. She devoted her life to her husband and his work. Nothing would prevent her from doing her very best for him. She kept a chart of each game at the University of Chicago, College of Pacific, and Susquehanna University. She kept track in response to those who wrote to my father—usually 40 letters a week. These were her works of love."[399]

## Chapter 21

# LAST WORDS

**H**ardin sat in silence, staring at the rock façade of the single-story building through the windshield of his rental car. He glanced over at the black sign with its stark white letters: Hillhaven Rest Home, 537 East Fulton Street.

He drew in a deep breath, exhaled slowly and opened the car door.

As he approached the building, Hardin tried to remember his last trip to Stockton. He opened the glass door and walked toward the reception desk, the smell of bleach filling his nostrils.

"I'm here to see Mr. Stagg. My name is Wayne Hardin."

"If you will go to the nurses' station down the hall, someone will take you to his room." The young receptionist smiled as she pointed over her shoulder.

"Thank you." Hardin spoke softly, wondering what he would find as he turned the corner.

\*\*\*

*"I'd like to be the team's kicker, Mr. Stagg." After weeks of internal deliberation, the freshman running back broached the subject with his head coach. "I know I can pin 'em back." The eighty-two-year-old Stagg responded without hesitation: "Kick it forty yards deep and high enough to give our men time to get down the field. Do that and you have the job. And I want you to use a one-step drop back."*

Hardin smiled, recalling one of his earliest conversations with Alonzo Stagg. The aspiring kicker spent hours adjusting to the rhythm of a rocking, one-step drop back motion of receiving the long snap and quickly launching the ball into the air. Hardin started as a running back and then, having proved his mettle, added punting to his responsibilities. The young freshman also stepped into the quarterback role as needed that fall. By his second year, he had become the Tigers' utility man—playing any role his coach asked of him.

Like most players of the era, Hardin played both ways. His speed and size positioned him well for the linebacker role he filled on virtually every defensive down.

The Grand Old Man insisted that as a team leader, Hardin set an example worthy of his teammates to follow. And when the boy erred, Stagg made his feelings clear.

*Hardin followed Jerry Carle's eyes as the Wildcat quarterback stepped under center and barked the play call. Pacific had failed to score on its first two possessions, and with barely seven minutes elapsed in the first quarter, the home team's sights were on a second touchdown. Hardin anticipated the pass, and the eager linebacker side-stepped to his left as Carle received the snap at the Tigers' forty-five-yard line.*

*Northwestern's right end, Ken Wiltgen, sprinted twenty yards toward the end zone and cut to the sideline. Hardin closed the gap on his man as the ball reached Wiltgen's outstretched hands. The Tigers' linebacker extended his arms and grabbed the sides of Wiltgen's jersey just as the Wildcat captain secured the football. Hardin forced Wiltgen to the ground at the twenty-two-yard line and, in his frustration, pulled his opponent's jersey over his head.*

*An angry Hardin silently cursed himself for not reaching his man in time to knock the ball away. As he jogged back to the line, John Rohde ran in from the Tigers' bench, yelling and signaling that he was coming in as a sub. "Hardin! The Old Man has something to say to you. You better get over there." The words hit Hardin like a punch in the gut.*

*The chastened linebacker dropped his head and walked to the sideline and his waiting coach.*

*"Wayne, I taught you better than that," Stagg said matter-of-factly. Hardin waited in silence for the lecture to continue.*

*"I'm sorry, Mr. Stagg." Hardin removed his leather helmet, knowing his day on the field had ended.*

*Stagg stared out onto the field. "Send John back out. And watch that right back." A confused Hardin looked at his coach, who responded, "Get out there. You haven't finished the job yet."*

*Hardin sprinted to the line, adjusting his helmet as he yelled to the defense, "I'm back in. Get outta here, Rohde!"*

*Hardin stared at the halfback lined up directly behind Carle and flanked by the fullback and left halfback. Frank Aschenbrenner had plowed through the Pacific line like a locomotive in the Wildcats' first series, and Hardin was sure Carle would call his number again as Northwestern stood in the shadow of the goal line. Carle took the snap from center, dropped back to pass and then turned to his right and threw a lateral to a waiting Aschenbrenner. Wildcat fullback Ralph Everist blocked Pacific's defensive end Don "Tiny" Campora at the line of scrimmage, creating a hole for the fleet-footed Aschenbrenner. As quickly as the Wildcat star reached the opening, however, he was met by a Tiger linebacker looking for redemption. Hardin wrapped his arms around Aschenbrenner with textbook form and pushed him to the ground at the fifteen.*

*The jubilant linebacker popped up and hustled back to the line to the shouts of praise from his teammates. From the corner of his eye, Hardin saw John Rohde trotting onto the field, signaling that he was returning to the action. "Hardin! The Old Man wants to see you again."*

*"What now?" thought Hardin.*

*A deflated Hardin shook his head and ran to the sideline. "Mr. Stagg, did I do something wrong?"*

*"That was much better," Stagg said.*

***

Hardin stopped at the nurses' station. "I'd like to see Mr. Stagg." A woman in her mid-fifties lifted her gaze from the chart in front of her, revealing the crisp white pinafore apron covering her pale blue short sleeves.

"Oh. Of course. Are you a family member?"

"No, ma'am. Mr. Stagg was my coach at College of the Pacific."

"Are you aware of his condition?" she asked as she stood and walked toward the hallway. "He hasn't spoken in almost a year—since before Mrs. Stagg died."

"No. I didn't know that." Hardin approached the door and hesitated for a moment, wondering if the man who never missed any detail on the field would recognize him.

The nurse sensed Hardin's apprehension. "Just talk to him," she offered with a reassuring nod. "It's good that you're here."

Hardin opened the door and peered into the room. The Grand Old Man lay still in the hospital bed, layers of thin blankets covering his frail body. Pale hands dotted with purple and red bruises emerged from the sleeves of his blue cotton pajamas.

Hardin paused at the sight of the man he revered.

When Hardin arrived at College of the Pacific in the fall of 1944, his eighty-two-year-old coach jogged two miles a day and was not shy about jumping into the formation to demonstrate proper technique to a lineman who missed a tackle or a block.

In one of his favorite drills, Stagg would stand twenty yards in front of a line of players, holding a football high above his head. His whistle signaled the next man up to sprint directly toward the coach, with instructions to cut right or left only when Stagg dropped the ball to his side to indicate the direction. Stagg waited until the player was within inches of barreling into him to drop his arm. "I can't believe I never knocked him over. But, man, did I learn how to make a sharp cut," thought Hardin, recalling the oft-repeated drill.

Stagg had carried the moniker "Grand Old Man" for decades before moving to Stockton, but Hardin and his Tiger teammates rarely thought of the sixty-year age difference between themselves and their head coach. And to Wayne Hardin, he was never "The Old Man" or even "Coach." He was always "Mr. Stagg."

As Hardin closed the door behind him, a squeaky hinge roused the resting Stagg. He turned his head to the sound, but his cataract-covered eyes could not make out the figure across the room.

"Mr. Stagg. It's Wayne. Wayne Hardin." He walked toward the bed and pulled a chair to its side. As he sat down, the muscular young coach swallowed hard to clear his throat.

"How are you, Mr. Stagg?" Hardin grabbed the outstretched hand of his coach. Stagg smiled as he squeezed Hardin's hand and held it. *One hundred and two, and he still has a grip.*

"Mr. Stagg, it's so good to see you." Hardin paused. "You know, I was thinking about all those years ago when I met you for the first time. I was just a wet-behind-the-ears kid who wanted to play football. You probably wondered if I'd ever amount to anything."

Stagg squeezed Hardin's hand in silent response to his former pupil.

"'You aren't here to play football,' you told me. 'You're here to get an education.'"

"I was listening. I didn't want to disappoint you." Hardin paused. "I never wanted to disappoint you."

The men sat in silence. As Hardin stared out the window, a smile spread across his face. "I remember one day during practice my freshman year, Mrs. Stagg was sitting over on the sideline with a notebook in her lap and a pencil in her hand. The linemen kept telling me to go over and see what she was doing. I didn't want to. I was scared to death. But they kept egging me on. Finally, I realized I didn't have much choice. They were all older, so I guess I drew the short straw."

The Grand Old Man smiled.

"So I walked over to the sideline," Hardin continued. "And I said, 'Excuse me, Mrs. Stagg. We were just wondering what you were doing.'"

"She looked me straight in the eye and said, 'Young man, I'm just deciding if you start on Saturday.'" Hardin laughed. "I knew right away that she meant business."

The men again sat in silence, and Hardin noticed that Stagg's eyes were closing. "Mr. Stagg, I don't want to overstay my welcome. I just wanted to stop by and say hello." Stagg's eyes remained closed as he squeezed Hardin's hand and held tight to it.

"I can stay a little longer," Hardin responded reassuringly, deferring to his coach's unspoken request.

"So I guess I made the grade with Mrs. Stagg, because I got my start against St. Mary's," Hardin's jovial visage turned serious. "Those Navy boys sure put us to the test. I had seven punts in that game. But we didn't give up a single return yard."

The corner of Stagg's mouth turned up, and he opened his eyes.

"You were right on with the one-step drop," Hardin looked into Stagg's cloudy eyes. "We'd never have had the great coverage we did without it. It took a lot of practice for me to get the rhythm, but I knew that was the only way I was getting the job." The grin returned to Hardin's face.

Stagg coughed and tried to shift his body. Hardin reached for a pillow at the foot of the bed. "Let me help you, Mr. Stagg." The young man stood up and leaned over the bed, positioning his left arm against Stagg's right side as he lifted his frail body forward to slip the pillow into place.

"Is that better?" Stagg blinked slowly, acknowledging Hardin's deed. He reached for Hardin's hand and held it at his side on the white blanket.

For close to an hour, the young Navy coach carried the conversation. Hardin told Stagg about his young children—three sons and a daughter. He shared stories of Roger Staubach, Joe Bellino and Tom Lynch. He described the experience of coaching the Army-Navy game just days following President Kennedy's assassination, despite his great reluctance, because Mrs. Kennedy insisted the game be played. And he told his beloved coach about the son of one of his assistants, Steve Belichick.

"Mr. Stagg, you would love this boy. He comes to practice with his father every afternoon. He studies the film and breaks down each play. Every week one of our assistant coaches sends Billy a copy of all the plays we will use in the next game so he can study the schemes and formations. This kid can't get enough of it."

In between Hardin's stories, the men sat quietly as a window fan hummed softly in the background. The Grand Old Man of Football reclined against the pillows, his eyelids closed, still gripping the hand of his protege.

Hardin gently squeezed Stagg's hand. "Thank you, Mr. Stagg. Thank you for giving me a chance." Hardin cleared his throat as his voice began to crack. "Thank you for trusting that I would learn what you needed to teach me."

Hardin stood slowly and squeezed his coach's hand a final time. "It was good to visit with you, Mr. Stagg."

As Hardin approached the door to leave, he turned around to the sound of a feeble but unmistakably clear voice.

"Wayne's a good boy."

# EPILOGUE

**N**o other football figure even approached the Grand Old Man of the Midway for inventiveness; he was the game's Benjamin Franklin, Alexander Graham Bell, and Thomas Edison rolled into one."[400]

Alonzo Stagg was responsible for—individually or in collaboration with others—more innovations than any other person associated with the game of college football. Ironically, West Orange, New Jersey, claims both Stagg and Edison as its favorite sons. Stagg was born there the year of the township's incorporation; Einstein moved there in 1886 at age thirty-nine and lived there until his death in 1931.

Alonzo Stagg's numerous developments changed the game of football. He pioneered use of the tackling dummy, the huddle and padded goalposts. His teams were the first to wear knitted pants with buttons and jerseys with numbers. His 1901 Chicago team was the first to use a white painted ball in practice and to practice under lights at night.[401] At Stagg's request, the architects of Chicago's Bartlett Gymnasium included a dirt floor at one end to allow for indoor football practice and, in doing, created the first university athletic field house.[402]

He developed formations and schemes employed by his teams and promoted to prominence by others. Chief among them were the forward pass, the shift, the man-in-motion, the quick kick and the short punt formation. He also developed the Statue of Liberty, sleeper and shoestring plays during his early days at Chicago.[403]

He developed the raw talent of young men with little or no athletic background, long before the age of scholarship athletes. And he produced championship teams at a university widely regarded for producing Nobel laureates.

Each of the three universities where Stagg coached named athletic facilities on their campuses to honor the legend. High schools in Chicago and Stockton bear his name. The NCAA Division III championship game is named the Stagg Bowl, and the winner of the Big Ten championship game receives the Stagg Championship trophy.

The Grand Old Man of Football also invented tools that became ubiquitous in other sports, most notably baseball's batting cage and the trough around swimming pools.

He was a founding member of the NCAA, the Western (now Big Ten) Conference, the College Football Rules Committee and the modern Olympic Games. His University of Chicago teams earned conference championships seven times from 1899 to 1924, with four of those Maroon teams going undefeated.[404]

Without question, he changed the game of football and elevated it to a position of prominence when it faced a likely demise.

His rules for clean eating, daily exercise and abstinence from alcohol and tobacco distinguished him from many in his profession. *And they no doubt contributed to his outliving the vast majority of his peers.*

Stagg was often seen mowing the grass on the University of Chicago football field to ensure it was done right.[405]

He modeled a life of virtue, exemplified by his devotion of nearly seven decades to his wife and "best assistant" Stella. He refused to go into debt for any reason, saving for nearly two decades to purchase a home with cash.[406]

"God, help me to do my best," Alonzo Stagg prayed before each pitch during his five years on the mound for Yale.[407]

This was his life's mission. And it is the legacy carried forward through the men and women who knew him and his influence.

# NOTES

## Epigraph

1. Mark Vancil, ed., *ABC Sports College Football All-Time All-America Team* (New York: Hyperion, 2000).

## Introduction

2. Bob Considine, *The Unreconstructed Amateur: A Pictorial Biography of Amos Alonzo Stagg* (San Francisco: Amos Alonzo Stagg Foundation, 1962).
3. *Chicago Tribune*, October 14, 1931.
4. From interview with Amos Alonzo Stagg Jr. by Dominic Bertinetti, February 22, 1985.
5. Ibid.
6. Considine, *Unreconstructed Amateur*.
7. Ibid. Alonzo Stagg championed amateurism in college athletics and would likely have bristled at the notion of receiving any remuneration as a student-athlete.
8. *Jackson Sun*, August 12, 1962.
9. Vancil, *ABC Sports All-Time All-America Team*.
10. Considine, *Unreconstructed Amateur*.
11. Ibid.
12. *San Bernardino County Sun*, December 3, 1924.

13. *Chicago Tribune*, October 14, 1931.

14. Ibid.

15. Edwin Pope, *Football's Greatest Coaches* (Atlanta: Tupper and Love, 1955).

## Chapter 1

16. Robin Lester, *Stagg's University: The Rise, Decline and Fall of Big-Time Football at Chicago* (Urbana: University of Illinois Press, 1999). Although this "triple-dipping" presents a clear conflict of interest, there was no official prohibition against such practices at the time.

17. Sports Reference, "Chicago Maroons School History," www.sports-reference.com/cfb/schools/chicago.

18. Lester, *Stagg's University*.

19. From interview with Amos Alonzo Stagg Jr. by Dominic Bertinetti, February 22, 1985.

## Chapter 2

20. William Rainey Harper, "A Tribute to Amos Alonzo Stagg," November 19, 1904, Amos Alonzo Stagg Papers, University of Chicago.

21. Ibid.

22. John Greenburg, *The Grand Old Man: Amos Alonzo Stagg* (self-published, 2000).

23. Ibid.

24. Lester, *Stagg's University*.

25. Considine, *Unreconstructed Amateur*.

26. *Chicago Daily Tribune*, November 20, 1904.

27. Considine, *Unreconstructed Amateur*.

28. Francis J. Powers, *Amos Alonzo Stagg: Grand Old Man of Football* (St. Louis: Charles C. Spink & Son, 1946).

29. Lester, *Stagg's University*.

30. Greenburg, *Grand Old Man*.

31. *Casper Tribune-Herald*, April 13, 1960.

32. Greenburg, *Grand Old Man*.

33. Harper, "Tribute to Amos Alonzo Stagg."

34. *San Rafael Daily Independent Journal*, March 18, 1965.

## Chapter 3

35. Considine, *Unreconstructed Amateur*.

36. Ibid.

37. *New York Times*, December 13, 1890.

38. Pope, *Football's Greatest Coaches*.

39. Greenburg, *Grand Old Man*.

40. Tony Ladd and James Mathisen, *Muscular Christianity: Evangelical Protestants and the Development of American Sport* (Ada, MI: Baker Books, 1999).

41. *Indianapolis Star*, November 29, 1939.

42. *Canandaigua Daily Messenger*, January 22, 1937.

43. *Kansas City Times*, November 4, 1961.

44. *Binghamton Press and Sun-Bulletin*, February 11, 2001.

45. *Wilmington News Journal*, December 19, 1991.

46. *Canandaigua Daily Messenger*, January 22, 1937.

47. Encyclopedia Britannica, "Amos Alonzo Stagg," www.britannica.com/biography/Amos-Alonzo-Stagg

48. *Inter Ocean*, January 19, 1896.

49. Kansapedia, Kansas Historical Society, "James Naismith," www.kshs.org/kansapedia/james-naismith/12154; Lester, *Stagg's University*.

50. From interview with Amos Alonzo Stagg Jr. by Dominic Bertinetti, February 22, 1985.

51. Ibid.

52. Mark Fagan, "Naismith to Live On in Bronze," KU Sports, February 27, 2010, www2.kusports.com/news/2010/feb/27/naismith-live-bronze.

53. *Detroit Free Press*, January 5, 1936.

54. *Green Bay Press-Gazette*, June 13, 1936.

55. *Indianapolis Star*, August 8, 1936.

56. *Corvalis Gazette-Times*, August 14, 1936.

57. *Indianapolis Star*, August 15, 1936.

## Chapter 4

58. Considine, *Unreconstructed Amateur*.

59. Ibid.

60. Pope, *Football's Greatest Coaches*.

61. *Marshfield News-Herald*, November 11, 1938.

62. Lester, *Stagg's University*.

63. *Hartford Courant*, November 18, 1981.

64. Grantland Rice, *The Tumult and the Shouting* (New York: A.S. Barnes, 1954).

65. Sports Reference, "1892 Chicago Maroons Schedule and Results," www. sports-reference.com/cfb/schools/chicago/1892-schedule.html.

66. Ibid.

67. Lester, *Stagg's University*.

68. *Courier-Journal*, October 26, 1893.

69. Pope, *Football's Greatest Coaches*.

70. Sports Reference, "1893 Chicago Maroons Schedule and Results," www. sports-reference.com/cfb/schools/chicago/1893-schedule.html.

71. Pope, *Football's Greatest Coaches*.

72. Allison Danzig, *The History of American Football: Its Great Teams, Players, and Coaches* (Englewood Cliffs, NJ: Prentice-Hall, 1956).

73. *Saturday Evening Post*, October 23, 1926.

74. *Inter Ocean*, November 30, 1894.

75. *Ogden Standard Examiner*, January 24, 1954.

76. Danzig, *History of American Football*.

## *Chapter 5*

77. Lester, *Stagg's University*.

78. AA Stagg letter to Pauline Stagg (sister), January 27, 1891.

79. Stanford has no official mascot, but its nickname is the Cardinal—in reference to one of the school colors. The first recorded use of the name was on March 19, 1891, when Stanford beat Cal in the first "Big Game." Stanford, "What Is the History of Stanford's Mascot and Nickname?" www.gostanford.com/sports/2013/4/17/208445366.aspx.

80. Amos Alonzo Stagg Papers, Box 18, Folder 6, Special Collections Research Center, University of Chicago Library.

81. *Salt Lake Herald*, January 2, 1895.

82. Greenburg, *Grand Old Man*.

83. *San Francisco Call*, December 24, 1894.

84. Ibid.

85. Lester, *Stagg's University*.

86. *San Francisco Call*, December 24, 1894.

87. The first football contest between Stanford and the University of California was played on March 19, 1892, at the neutral site of San Francisco's Haight Street Grounds. According to tradition, the game's

start was delayed for an hour as officials looked for a ball. *Santa Cruz Sentinel*, November 21, 1997.

88. *Fresno Morning Republican*, March 1, 1895.

89. Greenburg, *Grand Old Man*.

90. *New York Herald*, December 26, 1894.

91. *San Francisco Call*, December 24, 1894.

92. Ibid., December 24, 1894.

93. *Daily Inter Ocean*, December 26, 1894.

94. *Daily Capital Journal*, December 24, 1956.

95. *Savannah Morning News*, September 10, 1939.

96. Ibid.

97. *San Francisco Call*, December 31, 1894.

98. *Los Angeles Times*, January 2, 1895.

99. Lester, *Stagg's University*; Greenburg, *Grand Old Man*.

100. Lester, *Stagg's University*.

101. Ibid.

102. *Salt Lake Herald*, December 4, 1896.

# *Chapter 6*

103. Big Ten, "Big Ten History," bigten.org/sports/2018/6/6/trads-big10-trads-html.aspx.

104. Sports Reference, "Big Ten Conference," www.sports-reference.com/cfb/conferences/big-ten. Michigan State joined the conference in 1953, and the ten-member league remained unchanged until 1993 with the addition of Penn State. The University of Nebraska joined the conference in 2011, at which time it was split into two divisions. In 2014, the conference expanded to fourteen teams with the additions of Rutgers and the University of Maryland. The East and West division champions compete for the Stagg Championship trophy on the first Saturday of December every year.

105. Ibid.

106. Lester, *Stagg's University*.

107. Ibid.

108. Ibid.

109. Ibid.

110. From interview with Amos Alonzo Stagg Jr. by Dominic Bertinetti, February 22, 1985.

111. Robert Pruter, "Chicago's Other Coliseum," Chicago History, January 2012.

112. Ibid.

113. *Daily Inter Ocean*, November 27, 1896.

114. University of Notre Dame, "What's in a Name? How Notre Dame Became the Fighting Irish," www.nd.edu/features/whats-in-a-name. Much debate exists about the first use of "Fighting Irish" in reference to Notre Dame's athletic teams. Likely, the name was not ascribed to the football team until at least 1909. Many schools of this era did not have monikers or mascots, and their football teams were often simply referred to as "elevens."

115. *Notre Dame Scholastic*, November 1, 1935, www.archives.nd.edu/Scholastic/VOL_0069/VOL_0069_ISSUE_0006.pdf; Danzig, *History of American Football*. Football's placement kick originated at Princeton University; thus, it became known as the "Princeton place kick." Prior to using the place kick for field goals, teams used the drop kick method.

116. *Daily Inter Ocean*, November 7, 1897; Danzig, *History of American Football*. Penn's John Minds kicked a place kick field goal in the Quakers' November 20, 1897 game against Harvard and was quoted as saying, "That was the first placement kick."

117. *Daily Inter Ocean*, November 7, 1897. At this time, a field goal was worth five points, a touchdown was worth four and a kick after touchdown was worth two.

118. *Notre Dame Scholastic*, November 1, 1935.

119. *Chicago Tribune*, November 26, 1897.

120. Danzig, *History of American Football*.

121. Ibid.

122. Lester, *Stagg's University*.

123. *Chicago Tribune*, November 30, 1900.

124. Pope, *Football's Greatest Coaches*.

125. Lester, *Stagg's University*.

126. *Chicago Tribune*, November 7, 1897.

127. The Nobel Prize, "Facts on the Nobel Peace Prize," www.nobelprize.org/nobel_prizes/facts/

128. Lester, *Stagg's University*.

129. Ibid.

130. *Indianapolis Journal*, November 29, 1902.

## Chapter 7

131. From interview with Amos Alonzo Stagg Jr. by Dominic Bertinetti, February 22, 1985.

132. Ibid.

133. Personal papers of Barbara Stagg Eccker, retrieved June 28, 2016.

134. *Inter Ocean*, April 15, 1900.

135. *Philadelphia Inquirer*, June 10, 1900.

136. Bill Mallon, *The 1900 Olympic Games: Results for All Competitors in All Events with Commentary* (Jefferson, NC: McFarland, 1998).

137. Ibid.

138. Sports Reference, "1900 Paris Summer Games," www.sports-reference.com/olympics/summer/1900; GBR Athletics, "Olympic Games Medallists," www.gbrathletics.com/olympic/other.htm.

139. "Baseball and Other Contact Sports," www.jcs-group.com/sports/personified/olympic.html.

140. Lester, *Stagg's University*.

141. *Chicago Tribune*, November 30, 1900; Pope, *Football's Greatest Coaches*.

142. Danzig, *History of American Football*.

143. Ibid.

144. *Chicago Tribune*, November 30, 1900.

145. Danzig, *History of American Football*.

146. Ibid.

147. Sports Reference, "Michigan Wolverines School History," www.sports-reference.com/cfb/schools/michigan.

148. *Chicago Tribune*, July 26, 1903; *Inter Ocean*, May 12, 1908.

## Chapter 8

149. Lester, *Stagg's University*.

150. *Chicago Tribune*, November 6, 1904.

151. John Kryk, *Stagg vs. Yost: The Birth of Cutthroat Football* (Lanham, MD: Rowman & Littlefield Publishers, 2015).

152. Ibid.

153. *Chicago Tribune*, November 6, 1904.

154. Lester, *Stagg's University*.

155. Ibid.

156. Danzig, *History of American Football*.

## *Chapter 9*

157. *Chicago Tribune*, November 30, 1905.

158. Ibid., December 1, 1905. The lone blemish on an otherwise perfect record was a 6–6 tie with Minnesota on October 31, 1903.

159. Sports Reference, "1900 Michigan Wolverines Schedule and Results," www.sports-reference.com/cfb/schools/michigan/1900-schedule.html.

160. Sports Reference, "1905 Chicago Maroons Schedule and Results," www.sports-reference.com/cfb/schools/chicago/1905-schedule.html.

161. Robin Lester, *Journal of Sport History* 18, no. 2 (Summer 1991).

162. *Michigan Alumnus*, January 1906.

163. *Chicago Tribune*, January 18, 1903.

164. Lester, *Journal of Sport History*.

165. Lester, *Stagg's University*.

166. Ibid.

167. *Chicago American*, November 23, 1906.

168. Lester, *Stagg's University*.

169. Ibid.

170. Greenburg, *Grand Old Man*.

171. Tom Perrin, *Football: A College History* (Jefferson, NC: McFarland, 1987).

172. University of Notre Dame, "Always 1 for the Gipper," September 2, 2015, und.com/always-1-for-the-gipper.

173. *Variety*, "Knute Rockne-All American," October 9, 1940.

174. John Sayle Watterson, *College Football: History, Spectacle, Controversy* (Baltimore: Johns Hopkins University Press, 2000).

175. *Chicago Daily Tribune*, December 1, 1905.

176. Ibid.

177. Watterson, College Football.

178. *Chicago Examiner*, December 1, 1905.

179. *Chicago Daily Tribune*, December 1, 1905.

180. *Minneapolis Journal*, December 2, 1905.

181. Army Navy, "Army-Navy Through the Years," armynavygame.com/sports/2016/10/4/army-navy-through-the-years.aspx?path=football.

182. Ibid.

183. Lester, *Journal of Sport History*.

184. Ibid.

185. Ibid.

## *Chapter 10*

186. Danzig, *History of American Football*.

187. Ibid.

188. Ibid.

189. Ibid.

190. Ibid.

191. *Boston Daily Globe*, November 24, 1892. Momentum-mass plays of three or more men, such as the "flying wedge," were banned in 1894. *New York Times*, May 9, 1894.

192. Danzig, *History of American Football*.

193. Tar Heel Times, "Tar Heels Credited with Throwing First Forward Pass," www.tarheeltimes.com/football/first-forward-pass.aspx.

194. Pope, *Football's Greatest Coaches*.

195. Danzig, *History of American Football*.

196. *Chicago Tribune*, October 21, 1906.

197. Danzig, *History of American Football*.

198. *Chicago Tribune*, November 12, 1906.

199. "Division III Football Records," fs.ncaa.org/Docs/stats/football_records/2017/D3.pdf; Division III/FBS: 7—Mike Prindle, Western Michigan v. Marshall, September 29, 1984;

"2011 NCAA Football Records," fs.ncaa.org/Docs/stats/football_records/2011/FCS.pdf, Division I-AA/FCS: 8—Goran Lingmerth, Northern Arizona v. Idaho, October 25, 1986;

"Division II Records," fs.ncaa.org/Docs/stats/football_records/2011/D2.pdf, Division II: 6— Steve Huff, Central Missouri. v. Southeast Missouri State, November 2, 1985;

"Division III Records," fs.ncaa.org/Docs/stats/football_records/2011/D3.pdf, Division III: 6—Jim Hever, Rhodes v. Millsaps, September 22, 1984.

200. Sports Reference, "1906 Chicago Maroons Schedule and Results," www.sports-reference.com/cfb/schools/chicago/1906-schedule.html.

201. Ibid.

202. Lester, *Stagg's University*.

203. Lefty Farnsworth, *College Football Historical Society Newsletter* (February 1990).

204. Lester, *Stagg's University*.

205. Ibid.

206. Pope, *Football's Greatest Coaches*.

207. *Chicago Tribune*, October 17, 1931.

208. Ibid., February 5, 1928.

209. Ibid., October 17, 1931.

210. *Pittsburgh Post*, October 3, 1907.

211. Pope, *Football's Greatest Coaches*.

212. Danzig, *History of American Football*.

213. Sports Reference, "1908 Chicago Maroons Schedule and Results," www.sports-reference.com/cfb/schools/chicago/1908-schedule.html.

214. Pope, *Football's Greatest Coaches*.

215. Danzig, *History of American Football*.

216. Ibid.

217. *Chicago Tribune*, May 13, 1906.

218. From interview with Coach Wayne Hardin, June 23, 2016.

219. *Minneapolis Journal*, November 8, 1906.

## *Chapter 11*

220. *Daily Arkansas Gazette*, August 13, 1908.

221. Ibid., October 31, 1908.

222. Sports Reference, "1908 Arkansas Razorbacks Schedule and Results," www.sports-reference.com/cfb/schools/arkansas/1908-schedule.html.

223. Pittsburg State University began in 1903 as the Kansas State Manual Training Normal School Auxiliary. The institution became a four-year college in 1913, and on April 21, 1977, Kansas State College of Pittsburg was granted university status and renamed Pittsburg State University. "Pittsburg State University: A Brief History," axe.pittstate.edu/_files/documents/PSU_aBriefHistory.pdf.

224. *Daily Arkansas Gazette*, November 15, 1908.

225. Ibid.

226. *Sooner Magazine*, "Tribute for Benny," November 1955, digital.libraries.ou.edu/sooner/articles/p9-10_p24_1955v28n3_OCR.pdf.

227. *Daily Arkansas Democrat*, November 13, 1909.

228. Ibid., November 14, 1909. Memphis's Red Elm Park sat on a hill, and this portion of the field lay on a steep ascent.

229. University of Arkansas, "Arkansas Traditions," www.uark.edu/athletics/traditions.php. The moniker "Razorback" was actually ascribed to the football team at least three years prior, following the October 1906 loss to the University of Kansas. While football historians may debate the origin of the name, the university's student body made it official with a

1910 campus vote to replace Cardinals with Razorbacks as the school's mascot. *Topeka State Journal*, October 15, 1906.

230. *Daily Arkansas Democrat*, November 31, 1909.

231. Danzig, *History of American Football*.

232. Ibid.

233. *Indianapolis Star*, March 7, 1910.

234. Ibid.

235. Danzig, *History of American Football*.

236. Sports Reference, "1910 Arkansas Razorbacks Schedule and Results," www.sports-reference.com/cfb/schools/arkansas/1910-schedule.html.

237. Pope, *Football's Greatest Coaches*.

238. *Chicago Tribune*, November 25, 1910.

## *Chapter 12*

239. Danzig, *History of American Football*.

240. Sports Reference, "1910 Western Conference Year Summary," www.sports-reference.com/cfb/conferences/western/1910.html

241. Pope, *Football's Greatest Coaches*.

242. *Chicago Daily Tribune*, September 25, 1913.

243. *Chicago Inter-Ocean*, November 6, 1913.

244. Northwestern's football team was known as the Purple until 1924, when *Chicago Tribune* writer Wallace Abbey referred to the team as "wildcats that had come down from Evanston" and "a purple wall of wildcats" following a hotly contested game against the University of Chicago on November 15. *Chicago Tribune*, November 16, 1924

245. *Indianapolis Star*, October 12, 1913.

246. *Indianapolis News*, October 13, 1913.

247. *Star Press*, October 25, 1813.

248. *Indianapolis Star*, October 25, 1913.

249. *Inter Ocean*, October 25, 1913.

250. *Chicago Tribune*, October 26, 1913.

251. *Indianapolis Star*, October 12, 1913.

252. Ibid.

253. Ibid.

254. Sports Reference, "1913 Chicago Maroons Schedule and Results," www.sports-reference.com/cfb/schools/chicago/1913-schedule.html.

255. Pope, *Football's Greatest Coaches*.

256. *Wilkes-Barre Evening News*, December 18, 1914.

257. Danzig, *History of American Football*.

258. *Los Angeles Times*, March 9, 1956; Pro Football Reference, "Paul Des Jardien," www.pro-football-reference.com/players/D/DesJPa20.htm.

259. *Morning Call*, February 6, 2005.

260. University of Chicago Photographic Archive, "Merrifield, Fred W.," photoarchive.lib.uchicago.edu/db.xqy?show=browse5.xml|1277; *Post-Standard*, June 25, 1910.

261. *University of Chicago Magazine* 8, no. 1 (November 1915).

262. Ibid.

263. The University of Notre Dame enrolled the first female undergraduates in 1972. Wabash College remains one of three all-male liberal arts colleges in the United States. Angela Sienko, "A Hardcover Thank-You Card," *Notre Dame Magazine*, Autumn 2007, magazine.nd.edu/news/a-hardcover-thank-you-card; Wabash, www.wabash.edu.

264. *Chicago Daily Tribune*, October 8, 1905.

265. University of Notre Dame Archives, "Notre Dame Football 1913," www.archives.nd.edu/about/news/index.php/2013/notre-dame-football-1913.

266. Ibid.

267. Jack Cavanaugh, *The Gipper: George Gipp, Knute Rockne, and the Dramatic Rise of Notre Dame Football* (New York: Skyhorse, 2010).

268. Danzig, *History of American Football*.

## *Chapter 13*

269. AA Stagg Collection (AA Stagg High School, Chicago), video interview of Dr. William O. Fisher, Superintendent of District 230, Chicago Public Schools; interview with Kristie Crisler (granddaughter), June 30, 2016.

270. *Statesville Record and Landmark*, January 15, 1959.

271. AA Stagg Collection (AA Stagg High School, Chicago), video interview of Dr. William O. Fisher.

272. *Akron Beacon Journal*, June 30, 1968.

273. Ibid.

274. *Rochester Democrat and Chronicle*, January 3, 1936.

275. *Traverse City Record-Eagle*, March 16, 1968.

276. Stella continued the practice when the Staggs moved to Stockton, California, in 1932. The University of the Pacific houses the collection

chronicling the legendary coach's life, with special focus paid to his fourteen years as head football coach of the Pacific Tigers.

277. From interview with Amos Alonzo Stagg Jr. by Dominic Bertinetti, February 22, 1985.

## Chapter 14

278. *Pittsburgh Press*, October 27, 1923.

279. *Reno Gazette-Journal*, October 21, 1933.

280. Garry Brown, "University of Chicago's John Schommer Was Basketball's First Superstar," Mass Live, September 7, 2012, www.masslive.com/sports/2012/09/university_of_chicagos_john_sc.html.

281. *Great Falls Tribune*, August 14, 1950.

282. *Journal and Courier*, September 26, 1928. Coach Stagg denied the assertion that he feared Purdue. "You know this cry, 'Stagg fears Purdue,' was framed by an imaginative newspaperman years ago. I never said it or hinted it. We've always had hard fights with Purdue and we respect its prowess. What this reporter should have said was that 'Chicago respects Purdue.'"

283. *Wisconsin State Journal*, August 27, 1944.

284. *Chicago Tribune*, October 4, 1908.

285. *Star Tribune*, October 29, 1946.

286. Harry Stuhldreher recalled his encounter with Coach Stagg in an interview with Stan Baumgartner of the *Philadelphia Inquirer* in October 1927. Baumgartner, who played on the Maroon football and baseball teams of 1912–14, could no doubt sympathize with the two young men on the receiving end of the Grand Old Man's wrath.

## Chapter 15

287. Sports Reference, "1920 Chicago Maroons Schedule and Results," www.sports-reference.com/cfb/schools/chicago/1920-schedule.html.

288. *Logansport-Pharos Tribune*, September 28, 1920.

289. *Ogden Standard-Examiner*, November 30, 1920.

290. *Chicago Daily Tribune*, September 11, 1921.

291. Ibid., September 1, 1921.

292. Ibid., October 4, 1921.

293. *St. Louis Star and Times*, October 23, 1921.

294. Ibid.

295. *Belvidere Daily Republican*, November 19, 1921.

296. Sports Reference, "1921 Chicago Maroons Schedule and Results," www.sports-reference.com/cfb/schools/chicago/1921-schedule.html.

297. Sports Reference, "1921 College Football School Ratings," www.sports-reference.com/cfb/years/1921-ratings.html.

298. *Daily Argus-Leader*, November 26, 1921.

299. *Bemidji Daily Pioneer*, December 8, 1921.

300. *Daily Pantagraph*, November 30, 1921.

301. *Appleton Post-Crescent*, March 17, 1921.

302. *St. Louis Star and Times*, June 5, 1922.

303. Pro Football Reference, "1928 Chicago Bears Statistics & Players," www.pro-football-reference.com/teams/chi/1928.htm.

304. Sports Reference, "1922 Chicago Maroons Schedule and Results," www.sports-reference.com/cfb/schools/chicago/1922-schedule.html.

305. *Standard-Union*, October 27, 1922.

306. Sports Reference, "1922 Princeton Tigers Schedule and Results," www.sports-reference.com/cfb/schools/princeton/1922-schedule.html.

307. Danzig, *History of American Football*.

308. Ibid.

309. Mark Bernstein, *Princeton Football* (Charleston, SC: Arcadia Publishing, 2009).

310. *Chicago Daily Tribune*, October 22, 1922.

311. *Standard-Union*, October 27, 1922.

312. Bernstein, *Princeton Football*.

313. From interview with Amos Alonzo Stagg Jr. by Dominic Bertinetti, February 22, 1985.

## *Chapter 16*

314. Larry Schwartz, "Ghost of Illinois," ESPN.com, www.espn.com/sportscentury/features/00014216.html.

315. Danzig, *History of American Football*; *Detroit Free Press*, August 21, 1946. Yost served as Michigan's head football coach from 1901 to 1923 and 1925 to 1926. He served as Michigan's athletic director from 1921 to 1941.

316. *Chicago Tribune*, November 9, 1924.

317. Lester, *Stagg's University*.

Original quotes:

Harold "Red" Grange and Ira Morton, *The Red Grange Story* (1953; reprinted Urbana: University of Illinois Press, 1993). (Grange)

Amos Alonzo Stagg and Wesley Winans Stout, *Touchdown!* (New York: Longmans, Green and Co., 1927). (Stagg)

Grange, *Red Grange Story*. (Camp)

318. Sports Reference, "Chicago Maroons School History," www.sports-reference.com/cfb/schools/chicago.

319. University of Chicago, "Jay Berwanger, First Winner of the Heisman Trophy, 1914–2002," www-news.uchicago.edu/releases/02/020627.berwanger.shtml.

320. Ibid.

321. Cory McCartney, *The Heisman Trophy: The Story of an American Icon and Its Winners* (New York: Sports Publishing, 2016).

322. Ibid.

323. *Chicago Tribune*, June 28, 2002.

324. University of Chicago, "Jay Berwanger."

325. McCartney, *Heisman Trophy*.

326. Ibid.

327. *St. Louis Post Dispatch*, February 10, 1936.

328. *Lincoln Evening Journal*, December 11, 1940.

329. Carol Felsenthal, "Mitt Romney's Chicago Connection," *Chicago*, July 7, 2011, www.chicagomag.com/Chicago-Magazine/Felsenthal-Files/July-2011/Mitt-Romney-Named-after-QB-for-Chicago-Bears-U-of-Chicago.

330. Lester, *Stagg's University*.

331. *Tennessean*, December 6, 1932.

## *Chapter 17*

332. *Fresno Bee*, September 8, 1933.

333. Wayback Machine, "Centre Football," web.archive.org/web/20091116160604/http://www.centre.edu/web/athletics/football/history_football.html.

334. Sports Reference, "Centre Colonels School History," www.sports-reference.com/cfb/schools/centre.

335. *Alton Evening Telegraph*, March 19, 1965.

336. *Los Angeles Times*, September 30, 1934.

337. *Dayton Daily News*, November 12, 1938.

338. *Des Moines Register*, November 13, 1938.

339. *Los Angeles Times*, December 22, 1946.

340. *Santa Cruz Sentinel*, December 8, 1946.

## Chapter 18

341. *Bakersfield Californian*, September 23, 1944.

342. *Fresno Bee*, September 21, 1944.

343. *San Mateo Times*, November 13, 1944.

344. *Fresno Bee*, November 19, 1944.

345. *Daily Times*, July 11, 1962.

346. CFB Data Warehouse, "All-Time Coaching Records," cfbdatawarehouse. com/data/coaching/alltime_coach_year_by_year.php?coachid=969.

347. *York Gazette and Daily*, May 13, 1959.

348. David Maraniss, *When Pride Still Mattered* (New York: Touchstone, 1999).

349. *Hagerstown Daily Mail*, May 8, 1959.

350. Ibid., September 24, 1959.

351. *Cumberland Sunday Times*, September 27, 1959.

352. *Lodi News-Sentinel*, July 23, 1959.

353. *Hagerstown Daily Mail*, September 24, 1959.

354. Ibid., October 18, 1962.

355. *Baltimore Sun*, October 7, 1962.

356. *Hagerstown Daily Mail*, October 15, 1962.

357. Encyclopedia.com, "Roger Staubach," www.encyclopedia.com/ doc/1G2-3407900533.html.

358. Ibid.; ESPN.com, "Notre Dame's NCAA-Record 43-Game Win Streak over Navy Ends," espn.go.com/ncf/recap?gameId=273070087.

359. Encyclopedia.com, "Roger Staubach."

360. *Frederick News*, November 27, 1963.

361. *Pittsburgh Post-Gazette*, August 28, 1962.

362. *Alton Evening Telegraph*, July 11, 1962.

363. *Danville Register*, August 12, 1962.

364. *Chicago Tribune*, October 27, 1946.

365. Ibid.

366. *Los Angeles Times*, November 24, 1946.

367. Robert Janis, "Whatever Happened to…Eddie LeBaron," *Washington Times*, May 29, 2008, www.washingtontimes.com/blog/redskins-fan-forum/2008/may/29/whatever-happened-to-eddie-lebaron.

368. University of the Pacific, "Football Legend Eddie LeBaron Jr. '50, Has Died at 85," April 1, 2015, www.pacific.edu/About-Pacific/Newsroom/2015/April-2015/Eddie-LeBaron-obituary.html.

369. Janis, "Whatever Happened to…Eddie LeBaron."

370. University of the Pacific, "Football Legend Eddie LeBaron Jr."

## *Chapter 19*

371. *Austin American-Statesman*, September 3, 1947.

372. *Pittsburgh Sun-Telegraph*, November 16, 1947.

373. *Chicago Daily Tribune*, June 1, 1955.

374. *Pittsburgh Sun-Telegraph*, November 16, 1947.

375. Jean Pierre Campbell, "Like Father, Like Son?" *Essence*, October 1996.

376. *York Gazette and Daily*, October 20, 1947.

377. CFB Data Warehouse, "1947: Coach: Amos Alonzo Stagg Jr.," www.cfbdatawarehouse.com/data/coaching/alltime_coach_game_by_game.php?coachid=4926&year=1947.

378. *Chicago Daily Tribune*, November 23, 1951.

379. Ibid.

380. *Public Opinion* (Chambersburg, PA), December 7, 1951.

381. Susquehanna University River Hawks, "Hall of Fame: James Hazlett," suriverhawks.com/hof.aspx?hof=91.

382. *Chicago Tribune*, December 31, 1951.

383. Chicago Cardinals, www.sportsecyclopedia.com/nfl/azchi/cardschi.html.

384. From interview with Ruth Eleanor McCorkill, July 17, 2016.

385. Susquehanna University, "Making History the Old-Fashioned Way," www.susqu.edu/about-su/newsroom/university-publications-and-media/susquehanna-currents-spring-2014/features/making-history-the-old-fashioned-way?page=3.

386. From interview with Ruth Eleanor McCorkill, July 17, 2016.

387. From interview with Amos Alonzo Stagg Jr. by Dominic Bertinetti, February 22, 1985.

388. *Mt. Vernon Register News*, August 3, 1953.

## Chapter 20

389. *Albany Democrat Herald*, August 11, 1953.
390. *Troy Times Record*, September 15, 1954.
391. *Chicago Daily Tribune*, June 3, 1955.
392. *Democrat and Chronicle*, August 17, 1958.
393. *Philadelphia Inquirer*, August 16, 1958.
394. *Baltimore Sun*, September 17, 1960.
395. *Sayre Evening Times*, August 17, 1962.
396. *Indianapolis Star*, August 4, 1962.
397. From interview with Wayne Hardin, June 23, 2016.
398. *Independent Journal*, July 23, 1964.
399. From interview with Amos Alonzo Stagg Jr. by Dominic Bertinetti, February 22, 1985.

## Epilogue

400. Pope, *Football's Greatest Coaches*.
401. Danzig, *History of American Football*.
402. *Chicago Tribune*, October 16, 1931.
403. Danzig, *History of American Football*.
404. Sports Reference, "Big Ten Conference," www.sports-reference.com/ cfb/conferences/big-ten/index.html.
405. *Tennessean*, November 24, 1924.
406. *Oakland Tribune*, October 25, 1926.
407. *Green Bay Press-Gazette*, January 24, 1959.

# INDEX

# ABOUT THE AUTHOR

*A*mos *Alonzo Stagg: College Football's Man in Motion* is Jennifer Taylor Hall's first book. Jennifer's larger-than-life Uncle George fueled her passion for college football when he introduced her to the game he played at Ole Miss in the 1960s. Long after his own children tired of listening to his tales of glory on the gridiron, Jennifer remained captivated. Her love endures, and she is thrilled to share the story of college football's pioneering coach Alonzo Stagg, the "Grand Old Man of Football."

*Visit us at*
www.historypress.com